GUERRILLA
PERSUASION

GUERRILLA PERSUASION

Mastering the Art of
Effective and Winning
Business Presentations

DON PFARRER

Houghton Mifflin Company
Boston   New York   1998

For information about permission to reproduce selections from
this book, write to Permissions, Houghton Mifflin Company,
215 Park Avenue South, New York, New York 10003.

Library of Congress Cataloging-in-Publication Data
Pfarrer, Don.
  Guerrilla Persuasion / Don Pfarrer.
    p.   cm.
  ISBN 0-395-88168-4
  1. Business presentations. 2. Public speaking.   I. Title.
  HF5718.22.P45   1998
  658.4'52—dc21   98-17998   CIP

Printed in the United States of America
QUM 10 9 8 7 6 5 4 3 2 1

Contents

Foreword

Every weapon and every concept in guerrilla marketing is intended to persuade, so it is natural and necessary to scrutinize the act of persuasion.

What makes guerrilla persuasion different from normal persuasion is the *awareness* of the guerrilla. He or she is aware of the situation, the person or people being persuaded, and the details of the act of persuasion itself.

Don Pfarrer has done a masterful job in this book of dissecting persuasion and making you aware of its every detail—for it, just like marketing, is a process and not an event. As with marketing, persuasion requires patience and insight. And as with marketing, the more you understand the intricacies of persuasion—and they are identified and classified in this wonderful book—the better you'll be able to persuade. Not only in marketing, but in everything.

This book will help you face up to and then conquer fear, one of the impediments to persuasion. It will help you realize that persuasion isn't something you do as much as something you and the people you are trying to persuade do together, an act of connection.

You'll see how important it is to touch personally the people you are trying to persuade, for they are part of the process. Successful guerrilla persuasion requires both a persuader and people to be persuaded. It requires emotion at its core even when logic and reason seem to be the only factors to consider.

Is painting a boat akin to persuasion? Don Pfarrer proves beyond doubt that it is—because both require preparation. A lot of preparation. Many people don't want to do it, but guerrillas know it is mandatory. If your boat hasn't been scraped, sanded, and primed, it won't be ready to accept the paint. If your prospect or audience isn't primed to listen, hear, and understand, they won't be ready to accept your attempt at persuasion.

As with guerrilla marketing, one of the names of the game is *relationships* because that's the essence of a connection and that's where persuasion takes place—not in the context of one person speaking to one or many, but in the context of their relationship. This book tells you exactly how to establish the kind of relationship in which successful persuasion flourishes.

In its soul, persuasion thrives on passion, the lifeblood of marketing, business, and life itself. Without it, marketing is listless, business is no fun, and life becomes boring. Without it, persuasion withers.

As you read these pages, you'll comprehend that persuasion is not a single action but a series of events, all connected, all aimed in the right direction, each picking up where the last leaves off. It's a continuing process that begins in your mind when you begin your preparation and doesn't end until it is also in the minds of those who hear you, who agree with you, who are persuaded by you.

Don does not let you confuse negotiation with persuasion but points out that negotiation is part of persuasion. And then he shows you how to navigate through the minefields of negotiating. He stresses the importance of *listening*, an activity not normally associated with persuading—unless you have the insight of the guerrilla. He explores the importance of looking and seeing to help you learn about those you wish to persuade.

Individuals and audiences are not passive entities. Instead, they have the power to accept or reject what you are saying. This book shows how guerrilla persuaders harness this power to gain acceptance, assent, agreement, and success.

Your own persuasion power resides in more than your mind. It is also manifested in your posture, your movements, your stance. You'll learn all the details of how guerrillas persuade with their physical actions.

The guerrilla persuader possesses five crucial character traits. Having four of the five just won't work. You must have all five and Don Pfarrer identifies each one so that you can summon the best that is within you to achieve your goals through persuasion.

Guerrillas are people with the power to make things happen. The name of this power is persuasion. Used properly, it may not be able to move mountains but it can move people, small groups or large audiences, to take the course of action you want them to take.

Are the best persuaders born and not made? The reality is that we are born with an innate persuasive ability—babies exercise it when they cry. The sound of that persuasion brings parents scurrying, ready to take an infant's desired action. But after infancy, one's persuasive talents fall off quite a bit.

That's why Don wrote this book. That's why I'm so delighted with what he says here. You're not a huge company with a gigantic support system. Most likely, you're an individual, an entrepreneur, a guerrilla searching for every edge you can possibly use. You may speak persuasively right now. If you do, you'll discover exactly what you are doing to be so persuasive, then you'll learn the keys to become even better.

If you do, you'll be transformed into a persuader of the guerrilla variety—the one who gives wings to his dreams. All it takes is the awesome power of guerrilla persuasion. That's what this book is all about.

Jay Conrad Levinson
Marin County, California

Preface

We are all persuaders by nature and by need. We begin our persuasion careers in the cradle, where we communicate our most urgent needs even before we can speak. Thus the first lesson we learn about life is that *we have the power to make things happen.*

This power takes a specific form, called persuasion. It always works in the same way, from the nursery to the boardroom. Persuasion is a mind-to-mind transaction in which the persuader/speaker sends a *message* to the listener. The message usually conveys facts. The listener receives this material and his mind goes to work on it. He sees or believes something new. This arouses an emotion that spurs him to *action.*

The baby howls. Mother or Dad hears the message and begins to feel the pressure. He or she picks the baby up, embraces it, and says in effect: "What can I *do* for you?" What action must I take?

This is the test of persuasive speech. It is effective, it works, if and only if it moves its audience toward action.

Even when the persuader's goals are limited — to win assent to a thesis, change an attitude, intensify loyalty, show that an opportunity exists where nobody saw one before — even in those cases when a speaker aims at an outcome short of action, her or his goal is to move the listener or dialogue partner onto the road leading to action. The test in the end will be the same: did the speaker make something happen?

In complex organizations divided by function and expertise (big businesses) the women and men who rise are the ones who make themselves felt, first within their own sphere, then across departmental and function boundaries. They do both by the techniques of persuasion, by *being* something more than a job-doer, by *projecting* their personality, and by *demonstrating* that their agenda is the right agenda.

The ability to persuade is the most conspicuous element in the career success of many conspicuously successful people, and it is the element most notably absent from the careers of many intelligent, talented people who never realize their full potential.

But persuasive ability is ten times more necessary if you are operating without the support of a big, rich organization, if you're working alone or in a small company, if you're an entrepreneur, seller, creator, or key person in a new, emerging, or changing business. In short, if you're a guerrilla.

In a guerrilla campaign you don't have a mammoth budget or a household name to back you up. The listener, whether potential investor, customer, or partner, isn't waiting to be impressed by a name like IBM or Merrill Lynch. That listener is focused straight on you, the speaker, and it is you that he will judge. It is your individual presentation and unique personality that will determine what happens in the mind-to-mind transaction.

Guerrillas depend for their business success on a set of abilities that make the right things happen. An entrepreneur raising money, a chairperson bringing a gabby meeting back to business, a caller leaving a voice-mail message, a marketing manager arguing for a price cut, a salesperson nurturing a relationship—whether or not they volunteered for the role, they are all persuaders.

And while it's obvious that some people persuade more effectively than others, everybody has a kit of talents and everybody uses the same basic methodology. Some are more aware of their techniques than others but every persuader relies on the Big Five.

My aim in writing this book is to show businesspeople, especially guerrillas, as clearly as I can *what they are already doing* when they speak persuasively. When we see the *structure* of persuasion—when we identify the forces that determine our success and failure as persuaders—then we can learn from experience and build our powers.

For that reason the book devotes a chapter to each of the five "drivers" of persuasion. Taken as a whole, the first five chapters amount to a sustained argument that the best way to develop one's persuasive power is to watch the Big Five working in theory and examples and to apply them consciously and tactically in real-life persuasion episodes.

The book doesn't try to sell a tool kit. I am not offering some novel, proprietary system to give speech to the mute. The Big Five are embedded, and have always been embedded, in human psychology and cognition.

What this book does is bring them out of the shadows, exhibit their interlocking powers, and show how they can be deployed, individually and together, in a persuasion attempt. That is the first mission of the book.

The second, woven like the first into the chapters on the Big Five, is to help the reader develop her or his powers of persuasion by showing how the five drivers are integrated into daily business life. A reader who watches the five as they go to work in the examples, who becomes thoroughly familiar with them, and who then makes them a more conscious and directed part of her persuasion technique in daily life will have gained everything the book has to offer.

It isn't so remarkable that we should be able to see these drivers in action; what's strange is that so few people consciously make use of them. Because this art is the lifeblood of business; this is the ability that cuts across all functions.

Here they are, the Big Five, the drivers at the heart of persuasive speech and of this book:

- Who you are—your "character" as a speaker
- Who the audience is—their power
- Your goals
- Your argument
- The skills of "pushback"

Whether you're preparing and delivering a formal presentation, speaking up at a meeting, or talking one-on-one in the office, street, or parking lot, the Big Five are the guidance system of an effective persuasion effort—character, power, goals, argument, pushback.

Sound instinct is a fine asset. Natural talent is great. Charisma is terrific. And experience is the best teacher. But to realize your potential as a persuader you need more than talent, charisma, and experience. After all, repeated failure or shortfall is an experience and we have all had it, however impressive our talents. In fact the failures we're most likely to repeat are those we're unaware of.

Particularly today, when so many of us do business with people whose native language differs from our own, we will persuade more effectively if our methods reach down to the rock-bottom fundamentals that the Big Five represent. Communicating across language and cultural differences requires an appeal to what's common to us all. The Big Five serve as the organizing principles of such an appeal.

What we need as business persuaders, in every case, is a way to leverage talent, focus charisma, and profit by experience. And awareness of the Big Five provides all of that and more. The Big Five give you a way to analyze success so you can succeed again, even in a *different situation,* and to understand failure or shortfall—when you don't quite make the best of an opportunity—so that the next time you will.

In a persuasion attempt, as in any business activity, you have to define your goals but you also have to see your methods clearly and know how they work. You are, after all, trying to create changes in a world that cannot be seen, heard, or touched, the world of somebody else's mind. What changes do you want? How do they lead toward your action goal? When, for example, does an *assertion* gain the status of a *fact* and when does the fact grow legs? A fact with legs moves and starts something moving in the mind of the listener. All of a sudden the here and now are not good enough; you and your listener feel an urge to go on, to go in some direction that feels like forward, to change, to act.

Since persuasion is an art, any book that's mostly lists of points, boxes, diagrams, and tips can never be much help. Nobody ever mastered an art by staring at funny little cartoons in a how-to book. But if you plunge into the middle of the *processes* of the art, if you put the Big Five to work in your speaking experience, you'll develop the power to *think independently* about each new persuasion opportunity as it arises. It won't make any difference whether you're selling a product, enlisting a partner, or turning a meeting in the right direction, you'll be a stronger persuader and a more effective and more appreciated colleague.

I write in the hope that this book will encourage creative, independent thinking about persuasion, because when the curtain goes up, *you are the show.* That's what it means to be a guerrilla in today's market. If you're looking at this book, you probably know the exhilaration of it already.

But the other face of exhilaration is fear, and Chapter 6 is devoted to the special problems of those who get butterflies in the gut at the very thought of giving a presentation or speaking up at a meeting. But not one chapter alone. The entire book will demystify the art of speaking to persuade and thus drain away much of the anxiety associated with it.

There are guerrillas who love to speak simply for the rush it gives. And there are others, equally intelligent, ambitious, and gifted, who have to conquer fear every time. For both groups and for the others in between, this book offers a tested, systematic way to overcome barriers to improvement.

A persuasion attempt is almost always going to be a pulse-pounding experience. Sometimes your hands may tremble; you may even feel the sweat streaming inside that fine new suit. And why not? Who ever said *action* should be boring? The thing is called persuasion because you are trying to make the right things happen in somebody else's mind. And why are you doing this? Because *something is at stake.*

And the stakes can be very high. The concluding chapter is about the intimate connection between persuasive ability and life success.

Nothing demonstrates the net present value of persuasion skill more clearly than this simple fact: speaking to persuade accelerates your heart rate. To say it another way: when you find yourself persuading somebody in business, you are always doing something that you define as important.

So if you're rich in talent, develop and improve it. If you think you're coming up short of your potential, find out how to do justice to yourself. And if you never gave a minute's thought to the whole process, it isn't too late to start.

1

Who You Are —
Your "Character" as a Speaker

If there's an acid test of the persuader's art, it's surely the ability to raise capital on the strength of a mere idea. As one entrepreneur described it: "You're selling air." You're saying to the man or woman with the money, "Give me some of that and I'll make us rich."

So let's start with this—with the challenge of an entrepreneur raising capital to fund a startup. It's the toughest example we could choose and perhaps the most instructive.

But if it's the acid test, what exactly is being tested? Is it the business plan, the market opportunity, or the entrepreneur and his or her team? We'll look at the problem from both sides, from the viewpoint of the persuader and that of the audience—the entrepreneur on one side and the investor on the other.

And we'll start with the audience, the listener. Specifically we'll start with Steve Ricci, a venture capitalist whose firm specializes in funding high-tech startups. Ricci's work is essentially a process of picking winners. How does he do it? In other words, *what does he need to hear* from the entrepreneurs who approach him for funding?

As he analyzes his firm's approval process Ricci seems to be reinforcing a lesson as old as the Greek philosophers and as fresh as the pages of today's *Wall Street Journal*: the keystone of the arch leading from idea to enterprise is the *character of the persuader.*

This lesson holds across all persuasion tasks. It is equally valid whether you're talking with a coworker in the privacy of your office or delivering a standup presentation to an audience of a thousand. And it applies up and down the ladder of organizational size and complexity, from the corner gas station to General Motors.

The "character" of the speaker means the whole galaxy of traits known as personality, but also something more. It's hard to say what this something is, but when it's there you recognize it. The combat metaphor is apt: when the night is dark and the enemy is advancing, would you want to be in a foxhole with this person? Does this would-be persuader have seriousness, "weight," reliability, dedication? Is she or he solid, *present*, real? Let's look at Ricci's selection process and see what it says about the function of the speaker's character in a persuasion attempt.

In a typical year Ricci and his partners scan six hundred business plans and proposals. They cull this mass down to about two hundred and invite the authors in for meetings. From among the two hundred they choose five or six to back with money. We'll pause a second to put our eyes back in our heads: five or six out of six hundred!

How can a kill ratio like that possibly represent a rational process? Yet it is rational, even in those parts of it that can't be expressed in numbers or algorithms. The point about business decisions, including investment decisions, is that they are not deductive. You can't decide whether to launch an enterprise by working your way through a syllogism or consulting an algebraic formula, although logic, numbers, algorithms and formulae often play an important role.

These decisions are wisdom decisions. They can go either way, and wise investors can disagree, each having a strong argument to support her or his decision. *This area called wisdom is precisely the territory where persuasion operates.*

So it's natural there should be many good plans that Ricci and his partners pass up for reasons that do not reflect adversely on the proposers. But what does Ricci's process say about the five or six persuaders who succeed at this fantastic job of getting money to transform an idea into reality?

As Ricci listens to an entrepreneur making a case he organizes his thinking within a triad. The three elements are: concept, people, deal. His job as listener is to find out how completely and convincingly the speaker addresses those points.

1) What's the idea, proposal, *concept*? What's the product and how does it find/create a buyer? What about patent issues and barriers to entry? 2) Who are the *people* behind it? What's their track record, education, intensity of commitment? 3) What are the terms

of the *deal*? Does the venture capital firm get enough control? Will future rounds of financing dilute the firm's stake? Can all parties agree on performance tests?

A venture capital firm's involvement goes much deeper than a bank's. The firm usually provides not only money to fund the startup but knowledge and guidance. The deal usually assigns the firm a degree of control, often in the form of a seat on the board. So the firm has to be convinced that all three elements of the triad are solid.

The triad is like a stool; it can't stand on two legs. One weak leg and it falls. If there's a weak element in the triad, the whole business plan gets tossed in the big pile with the other 594 rejects.

Suppose Plan No. 333 offers a great concept backed by an inspiring entrepreneur, but the deal is unattractive. Into the big pile! Or the deal is good and so are the people, but something's wrong with the concept. *Step down.* Deal and concept are good but one of the V.C. partners has doubts about the entrepreneur and his or her team. Farewell, No. 333.

To this point it might seem that the three elements of the triad are equal. But not necessarily. As Ricci goes deeper into his selection process we remember the old maxim that investors bet on the jockey, not the horse. What seems to be happening is that one element is spreading its influence to the others. The *people* element is influencing the investors' appraisal of concept and deal. We're reminded of another truism in the world of startups: an entrepreneur who has done it before, and done it successfully, has a much better chance of getting funding than a novice. What we are calling the *character of the speaker*—and that includes track record—is gaining in importance over the other two elements of the triad.

Consider, for example, that Ricci says too much technical jargon bothers him. "A person who cannot tell a story without using jargon probably doesn't understand it very well himself," he says. The engineering has to work, but customers buy benefits, not blueprints.

Or take this: "It's very refreshing and compelling when you find the executive who can build his logic step by step, who does it by coming into a world you understand." So apparently it isn't just their case that matters to this powerholder, but how they present it makes a difference too.

Another telling comment: good, succinct writing saves the reader's time and bespeaks a well-organized mind in the writer. "Conciseness reveals the capacity to organize, and that maybe implies something more fundamental about the thought processes of the writer and the quality of the thought processes." Crazy as it may at first seem, Ricci is looking at *style*.

"These entrepreneurs we're backing have a different view of the world. There's something new that they've seen. So you're betting on the validity of their judgments, you're betting their judgment is right, and when you do that, you want to feel you're dealing with smart, hard-working, insightful people." And good writing indicates clear thinking. Style and substance are linked.

But surely they don't make a multimillion-dollar bet on the basis of scattered impressions and subjective feelings? No, they don't. When they feel good at this level *they go deeper*. And if they don't feel good: Game Over.

"Going deeper" means rigorous reference checks but it also means long meetings, several of them, between the entrepreneur and all five general partners in Ricci's firm. What are the partners doing? They are assessing the whole triad but, more particularly, they are trying to judge how realistic the entrepreneur and his team are with themselves. The partners, being a diversely talented group, come at the proposers from many angles and apply a variety of litmus tests. Uppermost in their minds is the question of a future relationship: do they want to work shoulder to shoulder with these people for a period of years? Because a venture capital firm doesn't just throw in its money and wait for the phone to ring. It invests and commits itself to work in cooperation with the entrepreneurial team.

Here we've uncovered one of the nerves of the persuasion process. It is, as has already been said, a mind-to-mind transaction but also, in varying degrees, it's a person-to-person commitment. The next chapter will go deeper into persuasion as a kind of partnership, but in the present context what's vital is that the audience—in this instance the venture capital firm—is evaluating not just the message but the messenger. They are using their business brains and their imaginations too, trying to get a grip on the question: do I want to work with this man or woman?

Therefore the partners' decision to invest rests in some degree on judgments about the entrepreneur's personal virtues: honesty, perseverance, judgment, goodwill, patience, fairness, and even courage. These qualities count at every level of complexity and size, but they count twice as much in the arena where guerrillas operate. The guerrilla—whether he's raising money in his role as entrepreneur or not—is first and last an individual. He or she is judged, primarily, not as a member of a huge organization but as a person.

If we view the task of raising venture capital from the other side, the persuader's side, we see the same emphasis on character.

For example, Eric Giler wasn't always president and CEO of Brooktrout Technologies. Not so long ago he was, as he calls it, "selling air," going after venture capital to start manufacturing electronic voice messaging and fax products. His wife was building the prototype on their dining room table, and the day when Brooktrout would sell $60 million worth of product a year was hidden in the future. How was anybody supposed to know it would ever come? Giler's task was to convince the right people it would.

When Giler analyzes how he did it, he recognizes the sovereignty of what we're calling Ricci's Triad: an idea that will work, an attractive deal, and a good team. Giler made some other points, some of them pretty remarkable:

1. If you need money, you'll never get it.
2. You don't need them; they need you.
3. Your message has to be true and your offer fair—but *you still have to be an actor.*

When Giler elaborates on these statements, you can see exactly what he means, because as he talks he is, consciously or not, *projecting a persona.* He is himself, he's authentic, the real Eric Giler, the same guy who shaves and brushes his teeth in the morning, but something sets him apart from the ordinary. Anyone who has ever conversed with a first-rate politician, military officer, executive, or salesperson will recognize the feeling. Giler has *presence.* He is intense without tension; he's "there"—not just a successful man analyzing his success, but an actor in the sense that in telling the story he relives the drama of his struggle.

Just when you think he's forgotten you're in the room, as he seems to sink deeper into his recollections, his large sensitive eyes will swing around and you realize he's been doing all this for you; not just talking but living it for your benefit.

He's a small-framed man with an attractive, mellow voice that sounds as if it were coming out of a chest bigger than the one he's got. He has an ability to concentrate, and when a speaker concentrates on you, the listener, something good happens in your mind.

This business of doing two things at once—talking and projecting one's personality—is at the heart of the concept of "character" in persuasion through speech. For when persuading we must *say* something and *be* something, two jobs at one time. More accurately, we must say something and *be somebody.*

Let's summarize Giler's observations first, then see if they fit into this double framework.

Giler recalled that he once had a mentor with extraordinary persuasive powers. "He could convince anybody of anything, even if it was difficult to cost-justify. I was blown away. How did he do it?"

Not, as it turned out, by being an egotist.

"His point was that he was always looking at and listening to the other person. He didn't worry about what he was talking about. He thought the only way you're going to convince somebody is if you're as close to being inside their head as it's possible to be.

"It's like driving a car. You always pay attention to outside movement. He said that to me and I thought, 'I'd like to be that good.'"

It is things like this that make people feel, when they talk with Giler, that he's all there for the listener. He's not a speaker who looks over your shoulder for somebody more important or who displays impatience or nervousness; he focuses all his considerable intellectual and emotional force on *the dialogue.*

This makes its impression, and the impression is one that affirms the importance of the listener or dialogue partner, which thereby puts him or her in a receptive state of mind. It translates like this: if this guy thinks I am worth his time, he may be worth mine.

Does this fit with Points 1, 2, and 3?

Point 1: If you need money, you'll never get it. This amounts to a belief that confidence breeds success. Or in our context, an investor who sees that an entrepreneur is in need will probably turn away. But the entrepreneur whose demeanor implies, "If I don't get the money from you, I'll get it somewhere else," this person may be worth listening to.

Point 2: You don't need them, they need you. The investor, Giler believes, "wants to get rich." She wants a stunning return justifying her fee and strengthening her reputation. In that sense it's she, not the entrepreneur, who's in need. Here is another statement of entrepreneur confidence. Such confidence has to be justified by reality. If it's not, why are you trying to raise the money in the first place? And if it is, why not display your justified confidence?

Point 3: You have to be an actor. It's not enough to feel the confidence in your mind, your confidence has to be an overt force in the presentation or dialogue. *Justified confidence* is money in the bank. It lengthens your line of credit, so let it show. Obviously this takes talent and restraint, but the only talent it really requires is the ability to be your best self; not somebody you never were and never will be, not Napoleon or General Schwartzkopf, but you as you are at your best.

So Giler's analysis fits quite snugly into the double frame. He has a message and conveys it; but in so doing he becomes somebody special, because message and messenger are both critically important.

He knows there's something investors want to hear and he knows how to be sure they hear it. ("My talent is to make you hear what you want to hear.") And what do investors want? The whole triad *plus*. He knows what you want because he gets into your head, following the lead of his mentor. In so doing he pays tribute to you the listener, just as you paid tribute to him by entering into a serious dialogue about the deal. ("They want to talk to you. Otherwise they'd be wasting their time.")

What is all this but the foundation of a partnership? And why should an entrepreneur be "acting" if not to show the potential partner what kind of man he is? And if that man is prepared, confident, articulate, and "present," something exciting might happen, and in the case of Brooktrout Technologies Inc., something did. Giler got his first-round financing, and they don't make the circuit boards on the dining room table anymore.

We now have to take a look at the subversive proposition that a good persuader is an *actor* of some kind. And an actor is somebody who pretends to be who he's not. Does that mean you fake it?

Far from it. In fact the opposite is a fundamental truth of the persuader's art: *sincerity and honesty are critical to long-term success.* The would-be persuader who is found, early or late, to be a phony or a truth-trimmer is compromised forever, in business, the military, nonprofits, or any other endeavor. He is even suspect in the morally hazardous game of politics. So what is this acting all about?

Only this. An entrepreneur who submits a business plan to a V.C. firm (to stick with our acid-test example) hopes to set something in motion. If the firm is interested, things begin to happen and these "things" take a predictable form, and within the form people start to act in predictable ways. A *drama* begins. The entrepreneur plays a scripted role and so do the partners. They will be judges, interrogators, investigators (in the due diligence phase), and possibly future partners. A venture capitalist, who is, after all, deciding whether to invest somebody else's money, *must* play these roles. If he doesn't interrogate and test and judge, he fails in his duty to his investors. Likewise the entrepreneur has an assignment: the role of champion of his idea and of his whole team. If he fails to play it to the hilt, he fails to keep faith with his friends—and himself.

His responsibilities run in both directions—to his team, to turn in his best performance, and to the V.C. firm, to exhibit the business plan in its full potential.

Just as the business plan is a carefully crafted document that must cover certain subjects—manufacturing, marketing, distribution, financials, etc.—so the entrepreneur's initial presentation and later meetings with the partners have to satisfy predetermined expectations. As one senior executive described it, a speaker on such an occasion must be ready to "improvise along carefully prepared lines." There is a structure here—a beginning, a buildup, and an outcome that is often a life-changing event.

Here's an example of what we mean by structure. Let's say an entrepreneur makes an *assertion*. She says that Return on Investment over five years will be X. Nobody in the audience would dream of saying, "Great. Now we've covered that, so go to your next point." No, an assertion of any moment is felt by listeners as the prelude to an argument, to a well-ordered presentation of supporting evidence. The speaker *must* follow through or she loses all authority and credibility.

Hearing her assert that ROI is going to be X, the audience expects to hear it justified by evidence and argument. What do they expect over the entire course of her presentation? Here too we see that persuasion follows a dramatic outline. They expect her to *build a case*, just as Ricci said.

This may seem obvious, but I've listened to hundreds of speakers who were blissfully unaware that a persuasive presentation has to go somewhere, that the audience expects something besides information. A presentation has to create a feeling of motion, and the motion has to feel like *progress*. We as listeners expect one thing to lead to another. That's our "structure of expectation." At the logical level a speaker makes progress by supporting her assertions and then showing how they support one another—how a product's design yields certain benefits, for example, how the benefits will shape the marketing plan, how marketing dovetails with distribution. Ideally the case builds by moving naturally from one assertion to another. Even when that's not possible, the speaker has to create a psychology of momentum, a sense that objections are falling away and incentives are crowding the mind.

This momentum is the perfect analog to the mounting tension in a drama, and it proceeds from the same source. That source is the careful revelation, step by calculated step, of the possibilities of the situation. The babysitter will or will not rescue the child whose little boat is being borne away toward the falls. The persuader will or will not justify her claim on ROI. And if she does, the next phase is more intensely involving for the audience because more is at stake. Suddenly, when she supports her claim about ROI, this begins to feel like a deal we might like. Therefore the marketing plan or whatever she presents next becomes more vitally interesting. As the proposal moves toward viability the intensity of the listeners' attention and interest rises.

That's how cases are built and minds are changed.

So far so good. We have seen that a presenter is an actor in that she or he plays a role in a structured event resembling a drama. But actors also pretend. Does the effective persuader pretend to be someone she is not?

SINCERITY

This raises the subject of sincerity, which is one of those virtues that are vital to the well-integrated personality. Phoniness and pretense are destructive of sound personality. But simple sincerity may not always be just right either. Life is a bit more complicated than that.

Imagine you're on the women's swim team at Kenyon College in Ohio. You and your buddies swim, shower, study, and travel together and you're a pretty happy and mutually supportive group. There are women here who may still be your friends when you have children and grandchildren. You'd never dream of hurting any of them.

Until the coach schedules time trials. Then you go all out to make the starting lineup and nobody in her right mind would expect you to do anything less. The trials are a drama in themselves and each competitor plays her proper role. Everybody knows that in the end some of these women are going to be hurt, and for whose benefit? For yours, if you're a winner.

Who was the sincere woman you hope you are? The bright-eyed, smiling, considerate friend in the locker room or the goggled demon at the time trials?

Yes, sincerity is a virtue, but it's nowhere near as simple as many sincere people think. The life of business—nonprofits, journalism, the military, etc.—is a complex life in which the striving professional is called on to play a variety of roles. If the test of sincerity is:

Do my words reflect my feelings? It may be too simple to cover the complex demands of the professional life. The entrepreneur may be excited; fine, but she would be ill-advised to open her presentation by saying, as all too many business speakers do, "I'm really excited about this idea!"

Why express your excitement before creating a flicker of excitement in the listener?

Certainly she hopes the partners will commit to her business plan, but there is a right time to propose explicitly that they do so, and that time should be chosen carefully and tactically—not on the basis of the speaker's emotions but on her assessment of *the emotions of her listeners.*

There is a better test of sincerity: Am I working for the right goals? Are my goals honest and am I honestly pursuing them? A speaker who passes this test will be better able to adapt to the "acting" part of the persuader's job.

Did Eric Giler really need the money? Does a bear need berries? But we have Giler's explicit testimony on how he dealt with the need: "If you need the money you'll never get it."

PERSON AND PERSONA

So a persuasion attempt requires a certain kind of acting, but definitely not the kind where you slip into somebody else's personality. The savvy persuader recognizes that his or her own genuine personality is a prime asset. People like to deal with those who are genuine. Therefore the kind of "acting" that's called for is not a personality transplant but an *intensification of the persuader's genuine identity.*

In presenting his business plan the entrepreneur has to be himself because fakery is destructive of personality. But he has to be *his best self* and rise to the occasion.

He has volunteered for a persuasion task before a skeptical and demanding audience that has the right to expect his best performance; he must try to give it. This rising to the occasion carries the persuader a little beyond his everyday self onto a plateau of achievement where his own abilities may surprise him. Like an athlete under pressure he may surpass his personal best.

It is precisely this intensification that we mean by projecting a persona—as Giler does, for example. At the lectern or in casual conversation in his office he is equally at his ease. His self-presentation in both arenas is perfectly effortless and natural. But when he speaks —when any good persuader speaks—he senses the entire drama and plays his role to the utmost.

It's one of those paradoxes that make the world of business the complex challenge it is. Our personalities are fully realized, and they grow, only when we are willing to dare something that might appear to lie outside our usual range, to *step out of line* and aim our lives at some daunting never-before-experienced enterprise, to say "Go!" and then actually to go into some unknown territory where we face the encounter and *live the drama.*

By living the drama, you don't necessarily behave just as you have in the past. You are developing new abilities and extending your range. In the business life you're persuading in one way or another virtually all the time, because in business encounters you almost always seek to influence other minds to see reality as you see it. You do this without even knowing it. But there's a start to this process. *You don't cross the line until you're somebody they'll listen to.* Therefore your first and career-long task is to present *yourself.*

Do others see you as you want to be seen? If getting launch money is the pinnacle of the persuasion art, self-presentation is the sturdy lowland from which such pinnacles rise. And the two tasks lie on the same continuum: presenting your ideas and presenting yourself are jobs that blend invisibly into one another.

One of the investors who helped Giler on the first round summarized his motivation in three words: "I liked him."

Suppose Giler had had the very same business plan and product but the personality of a reclusive toad. Would this investor have opened his checkbook?

You need to be your genuine self—your integrity and peace of mind require it. But this person must be projected into the drama, and once projected he or she becomes your *persona,* your delegate, playing your role on your behalf. If this sounds mystical, it isn't. It just means you rise to the occasion with your best talents and energy. The person is you as you are in your mind; the persona is a character, one of several in a drama; and there's another definition: *the persona is the full realization of the potential of the person.*

The potential becomes reality under the pressure of the drama, which is a crucible of character development. Because you have to argue a case, you do it; because you have to deal with skeptics, field questions, explain the complexities, you do it.

This is how, by saying something, you become somebody. Because you are more than the messenger, you are the very heart of the message. Especially when you're a guerrilla/entrepreneur, your overall success depends so heavily on your success as a persuader that there's very little difference. The good guerrilla is a good persuader. A good persuader has an excellent chance of being a successful guerrilla. So let's now take a closer look at *you*, the effective persuader.

ELEMENTS OF THE PERSUASIVE PERSONA

The good persuader aims to arouse and reinforce a certain emotion in the listener. That emotion is a compound of *respect* and *trust*. Therefore the truly persuasive speaker, whether his audience numbers one or ten thousand, is one who projects certain character traits whose combined effect is to engender respect and trust in the audience. These character traits, when they move into action, are the elements of the persuasive persona. The list is simple and short:

- Subject Mastery
- Steadiness
- Ability
- Empathy
- Candor

You possess all these in varying degrees, and your task when you volunteer for a persuasion role is to develop and strengthen them so you can do justice to yourself and support your friends and allies as their champion. You don't have to be another Winston Churchill, Jesse Jackson, or Sandra Day O'Connor. All you have to do is call forth the best that's in you.

Subject Mastery

Since persuasion issues are decided in the arena of wisdom, not deduction, your listeners or dialogue partners will, to one degree or another, find themselves dealing in probabilities. Numbers such as market survey data, revenue projections, and such are mere quantifications of the unknowable. They aren't conclusive; they are the raw material from which experienced minds must fashion the conclusions. The best the numbers can do is to refine the probabilities and structure the decision-maker's thinking.

People make business decisions in a state of doubt. An executive who waits for perfect knowledge will be like General George McClellan who, in the Civil War, sat on a huge army waiting for more troops, more supplies, and better opportunities until Lincoln finally fired him and looked for a general who would fight. Opportunities don't last forever. That's the one certainty.

But in this state of inevitable doubt the most reassuring force is a thought-leader who knows the subject inside-out. So that's what the persuader must become, a thoroughly informed thought-leader.

She must master her subject and she must know the limits of her knowledge. Both are essential and both inspire trust and respect.

Steadiness

Because he is a thought-leader the persuader must learn to keep a steady hand on the tiller. He tries to lead his listeners through doubt to conviction, and thus implicitly states that he knows the destination and how to get there. So if he falters or wavers, he's slipping out of character. His role is to lead.

An entrepreneur must display a well-merited confidence in his enterprise. When questions arise about competitors, for example, or barriers to entry, he must show the calm and perseverance of one who has been over that terrain many times and is ready to take on the questions and lead the questioners confidently through the same paths he himself has earlier discovered.

He may have to change course to avoid a hurricane but he shouldn't let a mere squall deflect him. His task is to know the difference and to shape the best course to the destination he has chosen. A persuader who is knocked off course by a little puff of adverse wind, who visibly loses confidence under criticism, will be viewed as unsteady and therefore unreliable.

Ability

You cannot demonstrate executive ability in a presentation or by your performance in a persuasion attempt, but you can very powerfully suggest you have it. This is done in two ways.

The first is to offer a quick history of your achievements. Nobody presenting a business plan should neglect to do this, although many do. Forgetting this means forgetting an element of the triad.

The second way is to give a dynamite presentation, to turn a meeting by noticing something the others miss, to lead a dialogue by incisive and timely questions or assertions. These examples of thought-leadership, while they don't prove executive ability, clearly imply it. They show knowledge, boldness, quickness, initiative, and drive. And if you're a marketer or salesperson, they come very close to demonstrating your ability to do your job.

This kind of performance is the best antidote to prejudices based on gender, skin color, looks, size, or age.

More than that, it demonstrates the synergistic combination of intellect and personality that moves businesspeople, especially guerrillas, on to success. Giving a great presentation is more than merely talking and showing visuals. It is a performance drawing on pretty much the same array of talents needed to identify and exploit an opportunity.

Empathy

In a long, searching conversation on the persuasive persona, Barbara Piette volunteered a surprising observation. "I really like it," she said, "when an entrepreneur wants to know something about me."

Here we have a woman enthroned in the seat of power—Piette is a venture capitalist who holds the speaker's fate in her hands—who yet wants to see from the speaker precisely what you'd expect the speaker to want to see from her, namely, a sign of empathy. Surely she doesn't need it the way he might.

But Piette explained that what she needed to see was a sign of *the speaker's sensitivity to his audience.* Why should she care? The answer runs something like this.

Sensing the whole event from the listener's side, nothing is colder and more sterile than a totally self-absorbed presenter. A guy who sees the whole world revolving around himself simply doesn't live in reality. He can be and ought to be presumed to be a poor judge of people, and if the jockey-over-the-horse theory of investing is credible, then this is a pretty ominous sign. Moreover, an egotist, even a genius, is an unpromising candidate for the kind of partnership an investor like Piette contemplates.

But it goes deeper. An entrepreneur who is interested only in himself suffers from an intellectual deficiency on two counts: first, he acts as if he were the most important person in the world, and he's mistaken; and second, he misconstrues the relation between speaker and audience. He thinks he's the only one who matters. This is no way to do the persuader's job, which is to start something going in the other's mind. This requires a means of getting close to that mind in the first place. And one moves toward the other's mind by both intellectual and psychological means.

In short the egotist acts as if persuasion relied on deduction. Show the audience your premises, he seems to think, and they'll inevitably draw the same conclusions you do. This is a grave error. In nondeductive reasoning, people can assent to a speaker's premises and refuse his conclusions. They can even agree with his conclusions and still refuse to have anything to do with his enterprise.

Candor

Claiming or implying that you know everything—even everything about your profession—is the egotist's mistake and earns the egotist's reward of contemptuous distrust. Nobody knows everything and everybody knows it. That's why candor is a feature of the persuasive persona.

Speakers sometimes fail the test of candor merely by omitting what they ought to include. Robert W. Kent, former head of management communication at Harvard Business School, calls this the mistake of forgetting to mention the dark side of the moon. When presenting a business plan, speakers often sail blithely on as if absolutely nothing could ever go wrong. Competition, patent issues, government regulation—all such issues somehow get left out of the presentation as if the moon had only one side—the bright one.

You may not have time in a meeting or presentation to give the dark side the full attention it deserves, but you have to say enough to accomplish three interim goals:

1. Show you are aware of the problems and hazards.
2. Suggest solutions.
3. Make yourself available for a full discussion at the next meeting.

Candor can be overdone. If you admit right and left that you don't know this and don't know that, pretty soon they start wondering what you do know. You can avoid this hazard in the preparation stage by carefully examining the whole subject and determining what's relevant and what's not. Then instead of overapologizing by saying "I don't know" too often, you can, where appropriate, say "We don't see that as a problem," and explain why it's not relevant.

There is no need to apologize for not knowing what you don't need to know. In fact there's no need to apologize for ignorance at all, unless it's ignorance within your core competency. And avoiding this is part of the presenter's job; it's part of Subject Mastery.

THE INTENSIFIED YOU

This then is the persona you project into the persuasion drama; this is the "character" who represents you *and is you* in the attempt to initiate changes in the minds of your listeners. This character is a task-oriented, turned-on, intensified version of yourself. His or her basic elements are:

- *Subject Mastery*—knowledge and interpretive capacity
- *Steadiness*—being calm and persevering under fire
- *Ability*—competence ranging over the whole opportunity
- *Empathy*—being a human person among other humans
- *Candor*—intellectual honesty

The listener may or may not register each of these separately. That isn't important. What matters is that he or she feel the kindling glow of that compound emotion, respect and trust mingling, without which minds are seldom changed and action seldom initiated. We try to engender respect and trust in order to open the mind of the listener and give weight to our evidence and argument.

How to open the mind and make it receptive to argument is a matter for a later chapter. It is time now to look at a question closer to hand: *how to project the persona* we've been describing.

PHYSICAL PRESENCE

Even before you start to speak you make an impression with your body, so let's start there and go on to eyes, voice, movement and gesture, and dress.

I have a cardinal rule: *Let them see your body.* The physical part of you has an important function in a persuasion attempt and it's not to be beautiful; the function of the body is to be *there*. It's the ticket that entitles you to your rightful role in the drama. Imagine a decision meeting where all the participants are gathered around a table except George, who takes part via speakerphone. He can neither see nor be seen, and his voice comes in squeezed out of a box.

It is of course possible that George could lead the meeting by virtue of his rank in the organization, subject mastery, or some other advantage. But strip him of these and he's immediately handicapped simply because he hasn't stepped onto the stage where the drama is being played out.

Now suppose George walks in, physically, and we see him to be a most unattractive man indeed, awkward, ungraceful, and the opposite of athletic. Paint your own picture of an unappealing face and put it on George. He's still the gainer for showing up because presence, in its original sense of just being there, entitles him to a turn at bat. Being there places him on the same footing as the others whether he's beautiful or not, and he will get his chance to guide the meeting.

Now suppose that this physically unappealing man is, or seems to be, totally unaware that some people find him less than striking. He just doesn't get it. He's crazy enough to believe the meeting has been convened to make a decision on the merits of a project, and that his support of one proposition or another will help, not hinder it. By this attitude he says: "We are all players, including me." This is a potent statement in itself.

Then suppose he makes a point everybody else has forgotten. Suppose at the same moment he leaves his chair and paces thoughtfully around the room while speaking, either deliberately or unconsciously making his whole body visible to the group. Now let's emphasize that it's not an attractive body; it's too fat or too skinny, too short or too tall.

It makes no difference. Being in the same room with George's body predisposes the audience in his favor—not decisively, but just enough to help him gain their attention, which is his to keep or lose depending on what he does.

Let us now suppose that this unbeautiful person called George begins to exercise an unexpected influence on some of his listeners. They begin to feel a faintly approving, pleasant kind of pressure that they connect somehow to the presence of George because of, or in spite of, his body having paused just three feet away.

It turns out there is something agreeable in finding merit where the fashion of our times (and perhaps of any time) tells you not to expect it. Presence gains attention through basic human empathy. Being original, alert, helpful, or right gains approval because we are pleased to recognize merit wherever it's found and to affirm that beauty and brains don't always go together.

Now it happens that while pausing close to a listener George scores another point in the discussion. He now has "presence" in a new sense, the kind of presence that is not only seen but felt as an emanation of some kind of inexplicable power. What could be the source of it? Merely that he's "right?" Why does it feel more and more like a pressure to agree, a desire to believe that George's argument has special appeal?

The intellectual source of this personal power is undoubtedly that George is saying something that opens a new view of the matter before the group. But the most likely physical source of this "presence" is his eyes.

If a speaker's eyes reach you, if they seek you out from among the group and acknowledge you as a sentient and rational being; if they imply that *you are worth something* while simultaneously opening the speaker's own person to you; if his eyes *stay with you* for several seconds, up to but not past the point of tension, then that speaker has as good as touched you.

The body and the eyes communicate more powerfully than words (just as the timbre of the voice can accomplish what words alone can never do); and the power is all the greater for the way it eludes precise definition. Like music, the pouring out of the speaker's consciousness into the eyes and thus into the mind of the listener cannot be said to *mean* anything. What is the meaning of a melody? And yet we all say quite naturally that some melodies "move" us and "appeal" to our emotions. In making this appeal they somehow *make us want more.*

Having heard a musical theme early in a concert or movie, having heard a melody that captivates us, and having experienced the incomprehensible emotion it evokes, what do we want? We want to hear it again, to hear it varied and repeated.

The eyes of a speaker, especially in a meeting or face-to-face dialogue, sometimes have the same kind of effect. What's happening is that we are getting to know the person in a new and more intense way. He may be unattractive by conventional standards but having seen his body we acknowledge his human status, a status we share with him. That's the first step; we are ready to discard conventional standards. Having heard his comments we salute his intelligence; that's the second. Having seen his eyes, and having allowed them to come to rest on our own for a few seconds, we have been introduced to him in a new way through a very personal medium.

The interlocking gaze is a kind of opening gate. The parties may decide not to move closer; that depends on a number of variables. But what's certain is that they *cannot* go closer without first opening the gate of personal contact. Eye contact equals personal contact. It is the start of an interpersonal bond.

George might say the wrong thing, lose his concentration, or blow it some other way. He might not be able to follow up. But one way you gain a foothold in the sense of being *intensely there* is by looking at others with openness, concentration, interest, and discretion.

Don't hold it too long, but don't just flit from person to person either. Let each one see your eyes as if you were letting each one see your inner being. And briefly, not intrusively, seek to connect with them by offering your gaze as a means of two-way communication. If we can't say exactly what is communicated, we can at least say this, that a speaker who does this acknowledges his listeners' humanity and opens his own for them to see, and the listeners know it. You can do this in a larger crowd too. It is remarkable how nuanced and subtle your communication with a large audience can be when you use your body, eyes, and gestures in a harmonious presentation of self.

A presentation is words and music. Words are essential but never enough. If they were, the speakerphone would be a great medium of persuasion at a meeting. Never rely on words alone. Set your words to music—the harmonious blend of eye contact and body presentation.

Where you place your body and how you let it move in the listeners' field of vision is an element in this harmony. In general, don't stray any farther away than the room and seating arrangement allow, but never crowd your listeners. They are entitled to some territory and no prudent speaker will encroach on it.

If you are seated, keep your hands away from your head and face. Do not compromise yourself by seeming to block your mouth or eyes with your hands.

At a recent meeting of guerrilla entrepreneurs there was a man who was one of four experts analyzing a case. He spoke intelligently but couldn't keep his hands away from his face. He began with a fingertip touching his upper lip. Having managed to utter a few sentences in spite of this self-imposed barrier, he spoke for about five minutes in an unmodulated, nearly monotonal voice. Then up went the hand again in front of his lips, as if part of his personality wanted to hold back the other part.

A transcript would have revealed his remarks to be truly expert—intelligent and original. But the persona he projected to this high-powered audience of three hundred fifty hard-chargers was hobbled by ill-concealed self-doubt.

Let your head be erect (not stiffly so) and let it be the main point of focus in the picture you present to the others. If it suits your style to lean your head sideways on your hand for a while, fine, but if this really is your style, ask yourself how much is too much. Remember that the audience sees you as a picture. Keep the image clear and uncluttered most of the time. Let them see an unencumbered face and head. Why? Because this is a simpler and more impressive picture. It is an image of independent strength.

If you're seated and have stretched your arms out on the back of a sofa, your hand movements will draw their eyes. So be careful. If in this casual pose you move your hands, you'll see their eyes jumping from your face to your hands and back: not a good effect.

If you are standing, move at least a little, and consider making movement the norm rather than the exception in your style. If there's a podium, don't consider yourself chained to it. You are not. Be free; move calmly, casually, deliberately; move because it feels good and looks good.

The best arrangement of the room for a speaker is a U-shaped table. Then you can slowly enter the open space in the center, varying your address from one side to another, and turning slowly while letting your speech flow on. Do not be afraid to show them your back. They are curious about that too, and watching it as you speak to people across the open space gives listeners a feeling that they see without being seen. But keep it short; then turn.

If a fixed microphone inhibits you, as it always will, don't use it unless it's necessary or you're being taped. Check into these matters before you speak.

Assuming you are not anchored by a fixed mike, make your key points while moving slowly toward the audience. Pause and use your eyes. Reiterate the point while standing still, then move back to a chalkboard or flip chart and write or draw something to express the point graphically. But make it swift; don't turn your back on them in this situation for more than a few seconds.

Let your gestures accentuate your key points or express your emotions. Beware of pounding a lectern, especially one with a mike attached. And if you point, let it be in a nonaggressive style. Better not to point at all, except to the side (as to a chart). Remember that if you tick off ideas on your fingers people pay more attention to the ticking than to the ideas.

Let your gestures suggest energy and power—"suggest" implying restraint. In my seminars on presentation technique I try to show speakers how gestures express personality. We videotape a presentation and then ask the peer group to comment on the tape. There are no "best" gestures and no out-of-bounds gestures except obscene ones. Each speaker has his or her own persona, and the gestures are part of it. The only rule is that they must be natural.

Through gesture and other forms of body movement you are striving to engender the respect-trust emotion. It is therefore a general truth that natural, easy, calm, and restrained gestures are more effective than anything extravagant. As Jay Conrad Levinson wrote in *The Way of the Guerrilla*, "The cool shall inherit the earth." Respect and trust gravitate toward someone who is at ease with herself, without being cocky. But this too depends on the speaker and the setting. *You* are your best asset; let movement and gesture express your essential identity.

Exceptionally good-looking people sometimes face a special problem in that their very presence can make business seem dull.

This is not the place to explore the many ways that sex-awareness complicates business communication, but here's a simple maxim that may serve as a trustworthy guide through that thicket. The maxim is: remember that it will never work to stoop, cringe, withdraw, or cover your body in sackcloth. Never express shame or dress as if you feel it.

Whether you are male or female, handsome or plain, *your aim is to move the audience toward the respect-trust emotion.* This is very different from sexual attraction; in fact there is no correlation between the two. We've all known cases of handsome people who profited from the initial goodwill that most of us accord them. What happens then is that they go one of two ways: they disappoint their listeners by being less competent than expected, or they prove themselves, not by looks but by performance. In the latter case we usually forget their handsomeness—or at least it recedes in our awareness.

But let's be frank. Handsomeness in either sex is a blessing, unless someone is too impressed with his or her own gifts or overestimates their efficacy. Most of us would rather be good-looking than be George, but the Georges of the business world succeed too, and *they do it in the same way* as the good lookers: by using physical presence to advantage. An effective speaker will show the whole body for the simple reason that body, eyes, and gestures enhance sympathy between speaker and audience. Your physical presence amplifies your message and sends it deeper into the mind of the listener or dialogue partner. It broadens your appeal from the narrowly intellectual to the emotional.

One way or another we all respond to the present human being. Mere presence is not enough, but it's the prerequisite of the *presence* that means power.

Call your own number and leave a message, preferably an important one. Let the content of it pose some dilemma (should I quit my job, ask for a raise, launch a new enterprise, propose marriage) so that your passions are engaged, and let it be long enough to accommodate a variety of language and tone. Let it convey a question, an exclamation, a recital of information, an exhortation, a challenge.

Then listen to it closely, keeping in mind that the telephone flattens the human voice. The phone message will give you back a little less than your voice put in. Still you can make rough judgments about:

- pitch
- timbre
- reach
- pace
- variation
- intelligence

Your *pitch* may go up if you're excited. If you find in this experiment or at any other time that it goes too high and becomes shrill, the way to drop it down is to slow your *pace*.

If you're a man, beware of straining to sound super-masculine by dropping to an unnaturally low pitch. The voice has to be natural and the pitch one you can sustain even when you're not thinking about it. That's why a conscious sinking to the cellar may get you into trouble. The moment you forget, up goes the pitch to its natural level, and your previous low tones suddenly sound pretty silly.

If you find that you like the *timbre* of your voice, play it again and notice the other variables. Chances are you'll find that when the timbre is enriched you're not rushing or overexcited, and that you are varying pitch and pace. Doing these things you somehow produced the pleasing, distinctive, and throbbing tones that distinguish your special timbre.

Reach is hard to measure on a tape, so we'll take this chance to toss in a bit of wisdom offered by an actress. Her advice is to achieve reach by playing always to the balcony. This has a double meaning: play to the cheap seats, giving the best performance you can for those who can least afford it; and project your voice to the last and highest row in the theater. Whether you're speaking in a theater or a small meeting room, make sure you reach the last, farthest hearer.

But there's a footnote. Reach the last row *and no farther.* A speaker who is too loud sounds nervous and a little inconsiderate.

Pace and *variation* are the heart of voice presentation. Pacing means suiting the speed of your speech to the sense of your message. Don't rush through material that's hard to understand; don't go so slowly that they are thinking ahead of your delivery. Vary the pace with your own mood and key the mood to the content.

The other kind of *variation* is the change of pitch and timbre to introduce a pleasing complexity to your delivery. Nothing is deader than a monotone address delivered at an unvarying pace. The listener craves variation in both pitch and pace.

Intelligence in the voice means the proper intonation and punctuation. Place the pauses, full stops, and question marks where you would place them in a piece of writing. Avoid the fad of putting question marks after declarative sentences (I went downtown? I was run over by a bus?). Above all give your emphasis to the words that deserve it, the ones that carry the heart of the message. Compare:

"Lincoln finally fired him and looked for a general who would fight."

"Lincoln finally *fired* him and looked for a general who would *fight*."

■ ■ ■

To decide how to dress, consult your role in the drama. If they're all wearing dresses and suits, and your role calls for you to emphasize your affinity with them, you had better dress the same way unless, for reasons arising from the drama itself, you are expected to be different. But in expressing personal difference it's better to err on the conservative side than to shock everybody by stepping clear out of the culture. Business is after all a subculture, and its members are pleased to see minor departures from the norms of dress and speech. But big leaps tend to unnerve them. If you want to take a big leap, decide first what it is you expect to accomplish.

A farmer asking for a loan doesn't have to look like the banker across the desk, but he does have to look like a farmer who dressed to come to town for a loan. He should leave his boots and barn coat at home. The general rule is: dress as they do, except when you have good reason to dress some other way. Business dress is becoming more casual all the time. Stay a little behind the edge of the trend.

A businessperson who is able to achieve the *presence* we've been analyzing is in possession of a kind of power. A quantity of it is worth five MBAs and ten years' experience. It is precious stuff. Yet there are speakers who throw it away by talking kid talk or otherwise setting themselves apart from the real players by their language.

The language called Standard English is supple, adaptive, and vigorous. There is seldom any need to step outside it unless some highly specific purpose so requires. Standard English is the language of business in America. Mutilate it and you risk losing respect.

Suppose only a few in your audience know that "the reason is because . . ." is ungrammatical. Of these, suppose only half care. Suppose further that your audience is quite accustomed to hearing "I'm like, wow!" and other high-school expressions. (This is what they hear from their kids.) And suppose they have heard clichés like "gimme a break" and "the whole nine yards" so often they pass right through their minds and leave no impression whatever. Suppose all this and you still degrade your impression if you fall into these and other lapses.

Nobody can accuse Standard English of being hostile to new influences. "Grow a business" was considered an abomination only a few years ago and is now accepted. And the rules of grammar are much more flexible in the real world than in the schoolroom. But consider a word of caution: language itself is power. Of the four most powerful men in the world in the twentieth century, Roosevelt, Churchill, and Hitler were extraordinary speakers. (The fourth, Stalin, spoke in bullets.) If your aim as a persuader is to offer your vision of reality to another mind, to move that mind toward an acceptance of your vision, remember that besides physical presence, voice, eyes, and gestures, your principal asset is language.

It is a system of signals governed by convention, by accepted norms of usage. You need not be totally subservient to the conventions but if you ignore them you should know the reason why. See-wha'm-sayin'?

SPEAKER AND VISUALS

There's another convention, however, that deserves a more critical look. It is the custom of keeping the screen alight with visuals throughout a presentation. Visuals have some very important uses, which we'll cover in a later chapter; right now, since we're on "the character of the speaker," we have to ask what effect visuals have on the speaker's persona.

Let's return to our bedrock proposition, that projecting the persona is an effort we undertake to engender an emotion, the compound of respect and trust. How can a speaker do this unless he or she is intensely human and intensely *present*?

Obviously he has to convey essential information and demonstrate that he knows what to do with it (weave it into an argument or narrative); and this may well require some pictures, charts, graphs, and such. But if the screen is lighted all the time and the main burden of the presentation is carried by the visuals, what happens to the speaker?

He runs the risk of becoming nothing more interesting than a clicker and flipper. The charts may indeed be totally engrossing, but especially in that case the speaker has surrendered the spotlight to a bunch of inanimate objects—the charts themselves and the fancy gear that beams them to the screen.

A senior investment banker was invited to address a meeting of small-business people on the performance of a certain category of stocks. If ever anybody was given a golden opportunity to impress an audience of hard-chargers it was this banker. What did he do with it?

He started by dimming the front lights so the audience would have a clear, sharp view of the visuals he was getting ready to show. The immediate physical effect was to put the audience in relatively bright light and the speaker in deep shadow.

This is precisely the reverse of theater lighting. In a theater the audience is shadowed and the stage is lighted for the excellent reason that theater patrons expect to see a show on the stage. By dimming the proscenium the executive all but declared aloud that it was the visuals that were important, not himself. "I the speaker am so uninteresting it's not necessary that you see me clearly."

So an audience of more than three hundred entrepreneurs, venture capitalists, private investors, executives, consultants, engineers, and lawyers, who had trekked through the snowy night to see something special, were told at the very start that they were going to see their five-thousandth slide show.

Having covered himself with shadow, he proceeded to do precisely what was now expected, to show a series of slides and talk about *them*. As it happened, they needed all the talk he could give them. Some were graphs with three superimposed lines crossing and recrossing in a hopeless tangle as they wiggled upward and rightward. Some were what amounted to his notes, which he read to us, thereby putting us in the peculiar and boring position of watching a speaker reading his own notes as he plodded through a predetermined "speech." In short, zero spontaneity and zero improvisation.

What was worse, some of the word slides were as baffling as the graphs, so crowded were they with small type. They looked like the pages of a book seen at a distance.

Visuals are supposed to help. These were a labor. If he wanted the audience to read his material, why not send a newsletter?

But the worst thing he did was to keep the screen lit the whole time: speaker in the shadow, audience in the light. Incredibly enough, this is a pretty common practice among business speakers. Maybe that's one reason so many audiences are left in a temporary coma.

What did this speaker sacrifice?

Although he didn't seem aware of it, he lost a rare opportunity to *represent his firm* to an influential audience. One can only explain his conduct by guessing that he was thinking something like: "We are here tonight to talk about a category of stocks." That was his assignment. Never let yourself be defined by your assignment.

If the purpose of a presentation to an audience like that is as dull as "talking about stocks," something is wrong. The speaker should take a closer look *at the whole drama*. Had he done so he would have seen there was no drama at all, not in his mind. Had he noticed this, he might have asked himself whether it was worth going out in the snow that night. It wasn't.

But if he had said: "No, I'm not going there to show wiggling lines and dense type. I could do that with a fax. I am going there to show my firm's flag."

Now we have a persuasion challenge, and the challenge of course is to engender the emotions of respect and trust and connect them to the firm.

Why settle for a low-voltage task when you have the coveted chance to speak before a high-voltage audience? The best thing the banker could do with this opportunity was to show the audience that he, as representative of his firm, was deserving of our respect and trust. These are emotions the listeners will remember long after they forget the wiggling lines and dead numbers. *We remember emotions.*

And, of course, you do not engender respect and trust from the inside of a shadow. The audience wants to see and know you. Step into the light and *be there*.

They'll remember the emotion and they'll remember you.

ANOTHER MEANING OF CHARACTER

Early in the chapter we inferred that Steve Ricci and his partners would find themselves making rough judgments about the personal virtues of their entrepreneurs. An investment of venture capital entails a kind of partnership, and when we seek out a partner we search not only for ability but for honesty, perseverance, sound judgment, patience, fairness, and sometimes even courage.

In other words the character traits we want in a partner are somehow related to those that combine to make up the persuasive persona. The two lists sketch somebody you have reason to respect and trust.

This is not a coincidence. Rather it reflects a truth about the workings of human nature in business. We seek and are pleased by the society of able and admirable people. And when we see an able person and admire not only her ability but her other positive attributes, we are inclined to attend to her views with a sympathetic ear. We listen and want to believe.

Of course scoundrels can be persuasive; nobody who observes the course of American politics, law, and business would doubt it. But as soon as we find out somebody is a scoundrel we put him in his proper category and take the appropriate precautions. We go on guard. But being cynical is not a happy state; therefore we're all the more relieved and glad when we find somebody whose virtues are visible and solid.

So there is, after all, another and perhaps more fundamental meaning of "the *character* of the speaker." It is the sense in which "character" denotes a full complement of virtues. And since persuasion operates in the realm of doubt, where we are called on to make judgments of probability based partly on wisdom, the character of the speaker in this new-old sense rises to supreme importance.

The persuader is a thought-leader. She or he says, "This is the world as I see it. These are the opportunities as I see them. Do you see them too?" He or she shows the way to new ideas and hopes. Scoundrels do it by lies and deception, which are forms of persuasion using trickery. The persuader we have been describing does it honestly, by Subject Mastery, Steadiness, Ability, Empathy, and Candor.

And by humor too.

John A. Pope Jr., vice president and member of the executive committee of the company that runs the various Reader's Digest enterprises, is an accomplished, casual speaker and a man who knows how to chuckle.

He says: "I use a lot of humor in meetings. If people can laugh, then in a way they're buying into what's going on. Laughter is a social activity and if the boss gets you to laugh, you end up being on his side. It means you're all on the same team."

So don't be too solemn. Good humor, the ability to smile or laugh at what's really funny, is not only a sign of intelligence; it also makes business and life more fun. And it's one of the rewards of living a guerrilla's life instead of a bureaucrat's.

2

Who They Are —
The Power of the Audience

We now have a pretty clear idea of *who you have to be* in order to reach maximum effect in a persuasion drama. Whether the persuasive persona comes naturally or you work on it, understanding its elements will help you to improve both the persona and your projection of it.

The next question is: who are *they*? Who is this colleague you're chatting with in the parking lot—this crowd of five hundred at a Chamber meeting—this super salesperson you're trying to recruit—this partner who's bent on making a terrible mistake?

These people, called the audience, meaning those who listen, *are not mere listeners*, are not passive, and are not powerless. (If they are, you're talking to the wrong people.) They possess power or the potentiality of power. The persuader affirms this the moment she rises to speak. Otherwise, why is she speaking at all?

Her whole purpose is to harness their power. And "harness" is just the word, because when she succeeds, she and they will be pulling the same load in the same direction. Yes, they're your co-workers, friends, business associates, and so forth, but their cardinal point of identification in the persuasion drama is their power. Some have more of it and some less, but those who have none at all are out of the drama.

It takes a certain amount of audacity to invite these people to see the world as you do and to adopt your goals as their own, but it is a kind of audacity that begins in humility. You start with the humble recognition that your goals lie beyond your reach. To attain them you need help. In any given persuasion attempt, if you could choose your own audience you'd pack it with people who are *friendly* and who *have the power already* in their hands to help you carry out your plan.

'Since this hardly ever happens—since the friendly don't always have power and the powerful aren't always friendly—it is usually necessary to make the best of the situation and audience you actually face. That's what this chapter is about: how to analyze real-world audiences and turn them toward your goals.

THE POWER-BENEFIT HANDSHAKE

Start by looking for a power-benefit handshake.

Who in the audience has the power to do what? If it's a one-person audience, what can she accomplish that will lead on toward your goals? If she can do nothing by herself but has influence with others, that's power too. Does the audience have some kind of power when acting as a body, as committees do? Is this power executive or advisory? Who are the key people who might form a balance-of-power faction in the committee? Is there some individual in the audience who wields final power, a decision-maker?

We are speaking not of power in some abstract sense but of *power in relation to your goals.* So the next logical step is to ask what benefits you can hold out to those who can help you achieve your goals. John Pope of Reader's Digest argues that the persuader must show the listener specific and personal advantages and benefits— why following a certain course of action is not only better in some task-specific way but better for the listener personally.

Without a benefit there's no incentive—but benefits don't have to be as tangible as the kind venture capitalists seek from the enterprises they help to launch. In those cases the benefits are power, money, and zest. But when Pope sought to motivate an editorial team producing, for example, an illustrated book on the national parks, the chief benefit accruing to the team was pride. Pope also had the authority to award cash bonuses to high performers; but his basic message to the team as a whole was something like: do your work so well that you and the whole company will look on the book with pride.

Of course people have to be paid adequately and valued as human beings, but there's a true sense in which excellence is a reward in itself.

So the benefit the persuader offers is something of value, from money right on up through a scale of psychological and spiritual satisfactions including pride, friendship, camaraderie, and, one of the most potent of all, reputation.

We can now see the main girder on which all audience analysis is built: the power-benefit coupling. Bestow benefits right and left just as you choose, but the ones that pay dividends in a persuasion attempt are the ones you offer to people with power. Audience analysis is devoted to identifying and appealing to those people.

In the case of Pope's book team, they had the power of any platoon of foot soldiers — to give their best or something short of it. Pope was capable of offering the benefit by virtue of his leadership position. As chief editor of the company's General Books group he could influence budget decisions and thus support the team with photographic, research, and technical resources. He could strengthen the team with human talent, serve as its advocate at the corporate level, and help sustain its energy and spirit. These were benefits tangible and intangible that he could bring to the persuasion drama.

In short this persuader had plenty to offer, culminating in the benefit of pride in the resulting achievement; while on its side the team had the power to make the project a drive toward excellence or a mediocre flop.

Clearly what we are witnessing here is a persuader creating a *relationship*. The powers and benefits don't go flying off into the outer darkness, they link in a kind of partnership. And *this is true of all persuasion that succeeds*. The persuader who wins the day has in a manner committed himself to an enterprise or idea.

A candidate for president of the United States who mobilizes his partisans and then quits when the going gets tough has broken a covenant. At Reader's Digest, had Pope urged his team to its best efforts and then failed, for example, to replace people who left the company during the project with people of comparable or superior talent, he would have broken his covenant. He did no such thing.

He did his part, and the team stretched itself to produce the excellent and profitable product Pope had hoped to see.

The same principle binds together the formal and informal business relationships guerrillas rely on. Commitment and loyalty go both ways.

We've now taken note of a paramount fact about the relationship between a speaker and her audience. The speaker is trying to form a kind of partnership—we'll call it the power-benefit handshake—because nobody can do it all. The speaker has a *benefit* to offer in return for the listener devoting some of his *power* to the speaker's purposes. That's why a persuader seeks to persuade, to harness audience power to overcome some kind of weakness. Nobody can execute a business plan alone. A "business" means people working together toward a common purpose.

Even when a speaker's only intent is to instill a certain attitude or calm somebody's anger, he does it for purposes related to his goals. For some reason or other he *needs* the audience or dialogue partner. So we've recognized this initial need. Persuasion arises out of need.

We've also seen that the speaker's need and the audience's power connect. When this connection is consummated, the benefits offered by the speaker connect with the power latent in the audience, and the partnership of speaker and audience can move toward action. There'll be no action until benefits and power shake hands.

So far so good. But now we have to get more realistic about the audience. We haven't yet taken its diversity into account. I don't mean racial, gender, or religious diversity, but differences in initial attitude toward you, the speaker. We're now looking at a hell of a mess—which is exactly what a typical audience is.

THE SPLINTERED AUDIENCE

You analyze an audience—learn as much about it as you can—to locate the power and figure out ways to appeal to it. But what do you do when the audience is divided against itself? When some members are friendly to you, others are hostile, others indifferent, and still others uncommitted? When their attitude toward you may be complicated by agendas and alliances running at cross-purposes *within* the audience?

First, don't despair. You can never know everything about your listeners and you don't have to. What you need to do is approach the hidden crosscurrents with a sensible strategy.

Assume a "splintered audience"—an audience divided into factions—and model it in your head as if it had four parts:

- Friendly
- Hostile
- Indifferent
- Uncommitted

That is, friendly to *you*, hostile to *you*, indifferent or uncommitted to you and your agenda.

With this rough model in your head you're in a better position to speak to these people, better than if you simply saw them as a menacing blob.

We've taken a small but perceptible step forward. We're guessing that the model of the splintered audience will somehow serve us better than going at the audience as if we knew nothing about it at all. How does it serve us? By controlling *the psychology of the speaker.*

When we speak to a blob—when we see the audience as an undifferentiated mass—there's an acute danger that we'll speak mush. A speaker who thinks of himself as speaking to a blob is one who doesn't know who he's speaking to. He addresses some vague and generic audience, which, because he hasn't given them an identity, is pretty much like himself, perhaps too much like himself. Very often he looks at the faces in front of him without really seeing them. He has an out-of-body experience. He feels as if somebody else were doing the talking while he stands to one side saying, "Who *is* this guy?" and praying he won't do anything stupid.

You can suffer the out-of-body syndrome from pure fear too, and from other causes, but one major cause of it is not knowing who the audience is—failing to *identify your audience of choice.*

You often end up speaking to and for yourself. You plod on through a speech or presentation as though it were a purely mechanical task involving nobody but yourself. You just crank it out as though your only job was to turn the handle.

But if you put this model in your head, however conjectural it may be, it will *force* you to *choose an audience*.

Before you choose, carry the deblobbing process a little farther by tightening the focus.

The Friendlies, you're assuming, will give you the benefit of the doubt. They feel an affinity for you and your goals and are hoping you'll do yourself credit and solidify their friendship by *making the right assertions* and proceeding to justify them. This in turn would tend to justify their attitude of friendship.

The Hostiles wouldn't be at all displeased to see you fail. They fully expect you to say all the wrong things, make all the wrong assertions, and then fall on your face trying to advance feeble or irrelevant justifications. Whether their animosity is personal or is-sue-related they are predisposed against you.

The Indifferent faction simply isn't tuned in. Don't know, don't care. Probably not listening. Too busy or too lazy.

The Uncommitted is the most diverse group. It harbors people who have already made up their minds, people who by rights ought to be in the Friendly or Hostile cohort but for various reasons are affecting neutrality. The Uncommitted group also contains thinkers who have addressed the problem but haven't reached an attitude, let alone a decision.

Consider now *what happens to you the speaker* should you ad-dress one of these groups rather than the others.

Talking to the Friendlies may be too easy. Talking to the Hostiles may be too hard, may make you nervous or defensive. The Indiffer-ent will lack essential information and perhaps force you into a teaching mode. In the effort to bring them up to speed you may lose the others.

But what's the effect on your psychology as a speaker if you talk to the Uncommitted? More specifically, suppose you *address your appeal to the true neutrals* in the Uncommitted group.

You've no need to feel apprehensive about waves of animosity coming your way; nor will you be tempted to cut corners by assuming support where it might not exist. You'll have to construct your argument with the same thoroughness and amplitude as if you were addressing the bitterest adversaries, but you can speak with the self-confidence and ease of one who knows that his evidence will receive a fair hearing.

These differences are subtle but can be important to the speaker. Both consciously and unconsciously a speaker modulates his message and delivery to reach an audience. Therefore his concept of who the audience is can influence both content and delivery.

Speaking consciously to Friendlies, a presenter might be tempted to skip some of the premise material and go straight to conclusions. He might get self-indulgent and start spouting opinions. He's not likely to feel free to do this while speaking to true neutrals.

If he thinks he's addressing Hostiles he might hammer so hard as to arouse suspicions that he's protesting too much. Also his personal affect might be a trifle uncharming if he imagines himself speaking to dolts and enemies.

But he knows that within his chosen group, the true neutrals from the Uncommitted category, there are people who at least lean in a friendly direction; so he can hope for a fair degree of empathy. And even from the neutrals who lean away from him he can anticipate a quantum of patience and fairness. They'll offer a style of attention the Hostiles would deny him.

Adjusting our delivery to a specific audience is something we all do every day. You can hear these adjustments in the voices of members of your family talking to different people on the telephone. These adjustments echo the speaker's status in a hierarchy; they express affection or enmity; they are a record of past success or frustration—but most of all they echo affinity between speaker and listener.

Choosing the true neutrals in the Uncommitted group, with perhaps an added shot of awareness that some of the people stopping there have friendly leanings, confers the benefits of affinity without the hazards.

■ ■ ■

The helpful effects in the speaker's psychology are matched in the audience.

The speaker who chooses to address herself to the true neutrals places herself under a form of benign discipline. She can only hope to reach them by speaking in tones of moderation, patience, good cheer, and reason; so that is how she probably will speak and should speak.

Audiences so addressed react accordingly. They sense immediately that they are identified in the speaker's mind as autonomous, reasonable, and fair-minded people. The shorthand is that they sense they are respected. Their inclination is to return respect for respect.

What about the other splinters—the Friendlies, Hostiles, and Indifferent—and the covert partisans taking temporary shelter under the tent of the Uncommitted? What's the effect on them if you address yourself to the true neutrals, while encouraging yourself with the thought that this camp also harbors those with friendly leanings?

This is what I call "going on display." You consciously orient yourself and your presentation to the true neutrals, and as far as you are concerned it is they you are addressing. But you're aware that the other factions are still before you, and many if not all are listening intently, because *they appreciate certain characteristics in a speaker.*

What characteristics? The very ones your chosen audience has called forth: your tones of moderation, patience, good cheer, and reason.

Maybe the Friendlies would rather hear a pep talk and the Hostiles would rather hear you say something ill-natured or stupid. The fact remains that because they are human they react positively to traits suggesting a person of good character and intelligence expressing himself in a persuasion drama.

So the effect of your choice of audience on the other groups is also positive—with this additional dividend: they sense that you are addressing reasonable, uncommitted people and they tend to watch the drama as if they were spectators. You are "on display" to them and so they feel a sense of detachment that makes it easier for them to listen and evaluate.

If they're Friendlies, they enjoy seeing you vindicate their position. If they're Hostiles, they can listen and perhaps change without the stress of being addressed directly by somebody they regard as an opponent.

Going on display to these groups is the best strategy a speaker can adopt before a splintered audience. For the Hostiles he is a less tempting target because he's not openly belligerent, not attacking them even when he quite obviously disagrees. For the Friendlies he offers a chance to reexamine a position they already respect, and thus to reinforce their commitment. And perhaps the best way to engage the Indifferent is to offer them a show without insisting they buy a ticket. The message to them is: "I wouldn't dream of asking you for a commitment." This is just what they want to hear—and they'll listen to the rest all the more readily.

How might this model work in a simple case?

You're ready to make your move. The meeting has been brainstorming the price point for a new software product for what seems like an hour and there's been no agreement. But you've got a fact with legs, and you think you might realign the discussion if you can introduce it deftly. Your fact is that nobody has yet mentioned customer payback, the money that buyers of the product will save by substituting the new software for human labor.

The array of forces in the room is pretty clear. There's a High Price group, drawn mostly from production and finance; a Low Price group consisting mostly of sales and marketing people; and a diverse, cautious, Uncommitted group. There is no Indifferent group.

This is a small company and virtually everybody is present. The power is spread all over the room because everybody has some influence, but in the end one executive (called DM for decision-maker) will settle the question. How do you reach him? He's been listening, not talking, and you can't even guess what he's thinking.

Fine. You don't have to.

You favor a high price, so from your point of view the High group are Friendlies and the Lows are Hostiles. To keep it simple let's assume it's a congenial company and the disagreements are purely professional (in reality they are usually more complicated).

If you argue to the Friendlies, you throw away dramatic interest since there is no intellectual work to be done in Friendly minds.

If you argue to the Hostiles, you seem to set yourself unnecessarily against them; you make an appeal it's unlikely they can assent to, at least not readily and not without losing face.

You could press your case directly with DM but his silence suggests he prefers a spectator role at this stage. Either he's genuinely Uncommitted or he wants to appear that way. In either case he seems to think he'll learn more by listening. He certainly doesn't want to be the target of all the arguments and has implicitly refused dialogue for the present. He is all but inviting you to go on display.

So do it. Argue to the Uncommitteds (without singling out DM) in some such way as this:

"Barbara, I've been listening to your comments and it seems to me they present a fair and balanced picture. And I know there are others—Jack may be one—who are still weighing our options carefully, who think it may be too early to settle on a price point.

"And I agree. We should consider all the factors carefully. That's why I want to add something that hasn't been brought into the discussion yet."

Then you bring in customer payback, using whatever quantitative measures you can—and the more numbers you use at this point the better—and proceed to show that the *meaning* of the numbers is that the high price (the one that generates more revenue, which is the *benefit*) is a lot lower to the customer than the bare number suggests.

Arguing to the Uncommitted lets you make your case to those most sensitive to its impact. It keeps the discussion nonadversarial. It puts you on display to DM. It avoids a direct collision with the Hostiles and it positions you as champion of the Friendlies.

By "address the Uncommitted" I don't necessarily mean you speak to them and them alone. You *think of yourself* as addressing them; you shape your argument to appeal to them, in the way already described.

What you're doing is controlling, disciplining, self-guiding your presentation—including both content and style. But you should also take the whole audience into the sweep of your vision, make eye contact with everybody, and beam your voice to everyone in the room, especially at a small meeting like this one.

Is there a dark side to this moon? Of course there is. Each persuasion drama is unique, and you can't address the true neutrals in every single case or without regard to the characteristics of this *particular* audience. Listen to your instincts, and as you gain experience you'll learn to trust them. But certain dynamic principles of the art apply generally and are repeated almost every time. In a case like the one above it will probably, most of the time, be best to follow the strategy I've suggested.

But if you feel DM has reached a point of readiness or is hastening toward a decision, especially an adverse one, it might be best to address him directly. If the Hostiles are numerous and you doubt that the Uncommitted hold the balance of power, address the Hostiles. If the Friendlies seem to have a plurality but are badly mismanaging their (and your) case, rally them with an energizing argument. And if the situation is extremely volatile, if there's tremendous confusion and misunderstanding, it may be best after all to address the blob and help it to organize its thinking.

LEAVING THE MODEL BEHIND

The utility of the model is that it guides the thinking of a speaker who is *probably* facing a splintered audience. When you are in the dark about the composition of the audience, it's far better to take a chance on the assumptions implicit in the model than to address a blob or, worst of all, proceed on the hope that everybody's on your side.

The model after all is based on experience. Most audiences *are* mixed in their attitudes toward the speaker. Choosing an audience-within-the-audience will very likely have good effects on your psychology and theirs.

Much as I like the model, though, there is obviously a better way to proceed, and that is to *know your audience*. As you increase your knowledge you may find you can dispense with the model. But use it when they're a closed book or you speak on short notice and haven't time to learn who they are. If you can learn, do it. Nothing you do before you rise to speak will pay off as handsomely as learning everything you can, by every means available, about the people and groups you are trying to persuade.

After doing this you may still end up with an audience model comprising the four major factions of Friendly, Hostile, Indifferent, and Uncommitted. The new benefit will be that you'll know the faces and names in each faction. Instead of a set of night-flying instruments you'll have a daylight view.

You can then choose an audience on the same principles—i.e., choose the true neutrals for the reasons given above—because those principles are still valid. But you'll have a surer grip on your choice, whatever it may be, because you know the people.

If your audience consists of one person—say you're asking the boss for a raise—it's still helpful to scan the four basic audience factions.

Is he indifferent? Does he know your work? Does he care? Is he hostile—either from personal animosity or a super-tight budget? Is he friendly? Will his friendliness make a difference? Is he a true neutral (is he really open-minded)?

Some careful thought along these lines can help you prepare your appeal and set your tone. The better you know him the more confident you'll become in *trusting your instincts*. Do the intellectual work first, answering questions like these or recognizing that there are some answers you don't know; then move into the area where your instinctive knowledge of your listener and of yourself take over.

ASSESSING THEIR KNOWLEDGE

It's time to move to the business of gathering more specific and deeper knowledge of the audience. We started with a rough-and-ready attempt to locate power and assess attitudes. We set the goal of a handshake (benefit from the speaker coupling with power from the audience). All this you can and must do when you know little about them.

Now move to a more enlightened choice by examining the audience through two lenses: knowledge and emotion, what they know and what they feel.

It seems obvious enough—a speaker ought to learn as much about her audience as she can in the time and circumstances at hand. But realistically, why assess their knowledge?

To get five immediate benefits.

1) *You'll be able to speak their language.* The more knowledge you have of their knowledge the better. Knowing what they know enables you to aim your presentation and choose your language to make it familiar and convincing.

In some patent-law firms all the lawyers are engineers too. Imagine the difference, if you're an engineer-inventor, between speaking to a committee from such a firm and a counterpart group from a firm where the lawyers are lawyers only.

2) *You can perform in their league.* Pitch your presentation too high or too low and you'll irk them. Worse yet, you'll waste their time.

This is an offshoot of the language factor. How much do they know about the subject at hand? If you come in at their level, you create an atmosphere of mutual understanding from the start and can proceed directly to business.

3) *You can appeal to their experience.* Before you can draw lessons from their experience you have to know its broad, general contours. Experience and knowledge interpenetrate. As you assess their knowledge you gain an appreciation of their experiences.

Let's say you know Bob is an investment banker but that's about all you know. A scrap of knowledge like this helps, but it also raises the danger that you might form a stereotypical image of a purely intellectual deal-maker. Then just before you meet him a coworker tells you Bob has done three deals involving Employee Stock Ownership Plans.

This shifts the whole force field. Bob is a different guy now. You still don't know enough—you never do—but you've made a start.

4) *You can exploit whatever affinity exists between you and them.* This thing called affinity is smack in the middle of the persuader's art. Shared knowledge is one source of it. If they know a lot about the marketing problems of microbrewers, and so do you, it means you enjoy the affinity, potentially at least, of those who strive against the smothering influence of marketing giants like Miller or Anheuser-Busch.

Affinity is a feeling of attraction and closeness, often arising from shared experience. We'll give it a closer look in a minute.

5) *You can meet them, not miss them, with your argument.* To persuade you usually have to argue. (Not the same as quarrel.) We'll devote Chapter 4 to this process, and all we need to show now is that there can be no arguing a point without an agreed bank of knowledge.

Let's say you propose to the boss that he give you a raise, and, awkwardly enough, he wants to know why he should. One first step would be to find out if he knows your work record. If he does you can *interpret* it to show, for example, that you deserve more money. He might say, "Well, it's a good record, Smythe, but I've got six others just as good."

Now you've got to distinguish yours from the others', which involves you and the boss in the interpretation of yet another bank of knowledge.

With no. 5 we reach the heart of the matter. *Knowledge is the oxygen of reason.* Your boss will never see how reasonable your proposal is if he doesn't see the grounds for it. And you can't argue for it till you know that he knows where your argument is coming from. It comes from facts, knowledge, evidence. To present the boss an argument you must know what he knows.

For all these reasons, and especially for reason no. 5, you gather power in your hands as you draw a mental map of your audience's knowledge.

THE "METHODOLOGY" OF COMMON SENSE

As to how you find out what they know, there's no great mystery and no arcane methodology.

- Ask questions
- Read
- Go online
- Find an ally/channel and ask more questions
- Network
- Get on the phone
- Read
- ASK MORE QUESTIONS

It's as simple and as hard as that. You learn by turning over the rocks. When you think you've done it all, look around for more rocks.

Start early. If you've secured an invitation, for example, to present a case study—presumably your own case—to a consultants' and entrepreneurs' group, your first step is to learn all you can by all possible means about the group and its members. This knowledge will help you shape your presentation and clarify your goals in making it.

The more you learn about their knowledge, its kind, breadth, and depth, the clearer your thinking will become about what to present and how to present it.

GAUGING THEIR EMOTIONS

Emotion is coded experience. If we had no way to encode the lessons of experience, its benefits would be lost to us because we have too much experience to remember it all. When experience is meaningful we "encode" it as emotion. We retain the emotion as the record of *the meaning of the experience* long after the data of the experience are discarded by the memory.

A banker, for example, who harbors an unacknowledged prejudice against restaurant loans is not necessarily the slave of an irrational fear. Maybe he took a couple such loans to his supervising committee, pushed them through, then lost the bank's money and his own prestige when they defaulted.

It's because cases like this arise all the time that a business persuader has reason to assess his audience's emotions—reasons and incentives just as strong as those that compel him to assess their knowledge.

"Emotion" and "knowledge" are not opposites, nor is emotional motivation necessarily irrational. Emotion and reason work together or against each other or in a complex interaction you cannot hope to untangle. What's certain is that they never separate entirely, except perhaps in the processes of deductive reasoning, and maybe not even there.

So if your aim is to start something happening in the mind of the listener (and there can be no persuasion without this) then you have to try to gauge emotions too. The mind you are trying to influence is an emotion-driven system. Even in what looks like a purely intellectual exercise—A leads to B and thereby proves C—you may have to deal with a mind that rejects "A" for reasons you can never figure out—emotion-based reasons that even your listener may be unaware of. Thus emotions can steal into even the purest intellectual operations.

Whatever may be the nature of the mind's arbiter, it listens to many voices. Even when it appears to be acting rationally it has often made nonrational choices about which voices to hear and which "facts" to let into the argument.

Open yourself to the emotions circulating through the audience. This of course is easiest when the audience is a single person. But whether you're speaking to a person, a group, or a crowd, be attentive.

Respect the emotions as if they were legitimate. They often are the midwives of wisdom. Learn all you can about them. Be sensitive to spontaneous gestures and unconscious signs of tension, hostility, eagerness, and enthusiasm. Watch them. Listen to them. Exercise a little patience and charity. Your payoff will be impressive.

1) *You'll sense the presence of obstacles and resistance.* These will sometimes be insurmountable but usually you can make headway against them; and you certainly won't get anywhere so long as you're unaware of them. In fact you run the danger of stepping on a mine.

If an individual in the room is set against you because of a passion you have failed to notice, jealousy for example, and if this person has the power to block your proposal and discredit your goals, you're in trouble.

If on the other hand you sense the tension and guess its source, you can at least begin to make a showing to the threatened one that there's room in the organization for both of you. And suppose there isn't. Suppose that between you and him it's a zero sum game. It is still better to know what's going on—to see the whole drama.

2) *You can arouse or calm emotions.* If you sense defeatism and despair, you can inject spirit and hope—or at least try. If you sense anger, you can calm it.

In both cases the effort begins in empathy, which is the talent of *feeling with* another. Like all talents it is a gift from the gods, but it can be developed and strengthened by human effort.

3) *You can select benefits and incentives more rationally.* Knowing what they like, what they desire, fear, or abhor, you can frame your presentation for maximum appeal.

4) *You can adjust your own emotions.* If the room is seething with anger and you simply don't notice, you'll certainly miss the mark. But if you have a just appreciation of what you're walking into, you can steel yourself for the storm. You can buck up your nerve to defend what you believe in, or reconcile yourself to a scolding if that's what you deserve.

Your state of mind is a critical part of the persuasion attempt, and it must in some degree respond to your audience's.

If you and your listener agreed to down a snifter of brandy, your moods would move toward convergence. Let's say you started out bored and a little depressed and he was still jumpy from a stressful day trying to sell stocks over the phone. The brandy would soften both moods and bring you closer to conviviality. Alcohol is a lubricant of social life.

Human interactions in a persuasion drama have a lubricating elixir too, and it is called *affinity.* The jackpot of audience analysis is just this feeling that the other person is somehow like you—and it goes both ways.

Affinity is the emotional glow of shared knowledge, shared experience, and shared hopes. When that crusty old venture capitalist said of Eric Giler, a man some thirty years his junior, "I liked him," he was expressing not only approval but affinity in all its dimensions.

Imagine two men working in the same company who discover they both served in the same regiment in Vietnam. Or two women who used to work eighty-hour weeks for McKinsey before deciding to cut the cord and go to work for themselves. Or a woman and a man working in San Francisco who come from the same county in Iowa.

Such discoveries form the basis of future affinity. They rest on shared knowledge or experience and are richest in potential when they include an element of struggle or escape.

The search for the quality and contours of the listener's knowledge and emotions is a search for her history as well as her present. When it discloses a basis for affinity it opens the way for the kind of relationship a speaker seeks with her audience.

The dark side of this moon is that some people try to perform a loaves-and-fishes miracle with affinity. They catch hold of an ounce of the stuff and try to turn it into a ton.

"Oh, hey, you saw that ninety-nine-yard punt return in the Super Bowl? Wow, so did I! So sign right here, OK?"

SENSING THE AUDIENCE

To assess knowledge and emotion, to discover and encourage affinity, a speaker must *sense the audience*. The senses that a speaker relies on once the presentation or dialogue has begun are sight and hearing.

You're now out of the preparation stage and into delivery— you're on your feet and talking—*but you go right on learning about the audience* by sensing their reactions to you and your message.

We've said enough for now about *sight*. Your eyes communicate your personality, your willingness to see and appreciate your listeners as people, and your openness to a flow of subtle communication from them. Through sight you express yourself and learn about them. Clearly sight is a two-way channel, and clearly by *looking at them* attentively and sincerely you convey important information about yourself while receiving a flow of consciousness from them.

At first it might seem that *hearing* goes only one way: you listen, hear, and receive. You don't send. But actually hearing, like sight, is a two-way channel through which a speaker learns what's happening in other minds and communicates information about her own personality and attitudes.

This will become clearer as we look at the three styles of listening: *real, demonstrated,* and *backlash.*

Real Listening

The speaker who *really listens* engages in dialogue willingly and for profit. Whether by inviting comments during the body of her presentation, in a Q&A session, during a colloquy around a table, or in one-on-one exchanges, she really listens because she wants to take the all-important step from statement to dialogue.

Of course people can be persuaded while they sit in silence. The listener's voice may rest but the mind goes right on working—absorbing, evaluating, revising, synthesizing. But a speaker who can encourage voiced expression of what's in the other mind (create a dialogue) achieves far-reaching and binding results.

The great utility of real listening is that it encourages a voiced interchange of thoughts. A real listener has by her own choice transformed a presentation into an interchange between equals. Whether or not the arguments are equal in merit she shows by her attention and responses that she believes the persons are. Once she held the floor alone and claimed all the attention; now she shares both with her dialogue partners.

Listening is real when the speaker opens the possibility of revising her own views under the acknowledged and justified influence of the other. The persuader has the confidence to declare herself willing to be persuaded. She has adopted the policy of the architect Jim Groom, a solo practitioner and thus a guerrilla in the true sense.

"The best idea wins," says Groom. "I don't care who thought of it." Like Giler's, this is a policy of self-confidence that speaks eloquently about the character of the person who adopts it.

A speaker who pretends to listen—at a meeting, say—but actually keeps a closed mind is playing a stupid game. It's far better to declare honestly that his mind is made up.

People who can't bring themselves to admit this are usually held back by a fear of being ostracized intellectually. They think, "If these jerks knew my mind was set in concrete, they'd think I was — well — closed-minded!" Nobody is supposed to be closed-minded, so the speaker fakes open-mindedness.

But why is it a disgrace to be closed-minded? It must be because the world is complicated and business policies and decisions require a bit of wisdom. So it's the closed-minded guy who's the jerk, not his listeners.

That is precisely why people sitting around a table to hammer out a new policy, for example, appreciate a willing, real listener. The world rolls along and changes with every turn of the wheel. And we are gathered here, dearly beloved, to *think*, to explore, and maybe even to revise our goals (more on this in the next chapter).

A speaker who is unwilling even to consider somebody else's views isn't some powerhouse of majestic confidence; he's a wimp and a chicken.

Therefore the real listener as we've defined him earns two kinds of reward. He *gets more information* because his dialogue partners open up to him, and he *gains their respect* for his confident reasonableness.

Demonstrated Listening

There is a kind of real listening that *makes itself apparent* to everybody in the room. Let's call it *demonstrated listening*.

It is real and *presented as real* by the speaker. She not only opens her mind to messages from the audience, including objections, but she demonstrates that she is doing so. She leans a little forward; she looks the dialogue partner in the eye with goodwill and purpose; she nods or otherwise signals her receptivity; she gives whatever time the format allows. And she may from time to time summarize what she's heard and seek confirmation. She is asking, "Have I understood you?" Doing this she lays down the knowledge base for the progress of reasoning.

Demonstrated listening is real listening articulated. It is real listening plus the self-expression that reveals to the audience or dialogue partner that you really are listening.

How do you do it? By words, facial expression, gestures of empathy and sympathy, patience, respect. Demonstrated listening convinces the audience that, whether or not you agree, you are weighing their comments conscientiously. This is all most audiences expect and all they are entitled to expect.

A speaker who is a real, demonstrating listener doesn't have to abandon her ideas and shouldn't. She is not in the business of buying a fleeting approval by giving up what is of lasting value in her life.

Rather she starts by formulating ideas that can endure scrutiny and challenge. She doesn't launch a leaky little vessel into a stormy sea and then run for the lifeboats. She builds a sturdy and seaworthy ship and launches it without fear of its being sunk in the first gust.

She says: "I welcome your criticism and your probing. Let's see if this idea is as strong as I believe it is."

Backlash Listening

Some speakers fall almost willingly into an adversarial relationship with the audience. As long as they can talk *at* them they're O.K., but the moment a set-piece "speech" takes a turn toward dialogue they show they have nothing to learn and everything to defend.

They slip naturally into *backlash listening*. This is a style of nonlistening in which the speaker's ears open just wide enough to admit one word of criticism.

To the backlash listener the first critical word is the opening shot of an ambush. "I'm being attacked!" He subscribes to Marine Corps anti-ambush doctrine: react instantly; gain fire superiority. He opens up with automatic-weapons fire before he takes a moment to think. Thinking is not part of his doctrine; it's too complicated.

Here's another true story of an opportunity lost.

The startup group at the MIT Enterprise Forum had convened for a dinner meeting. The forty members were seated along a U-shaped table with the moderator and four designated experts at the bottom of the U. The other members, arranged along the legs of the U, were experts too—lawyers specializing in the problems of startups, consultants, engineers, inventors, entrepreneurs, and investors. In the open market the panel alone would be worth thousands an hour. Throw in the expertise of the rest of the crowd and the number would grow to astronomical proportions.

The general audience would be commenting on the plans as presented, but the panel had also devoted hours to studying the written plans and accompanying exhibits. So it was a brilliant opportunity for the two entrepreneurs scheduled to present their business plans that evening.

Each speaker's hour was divided into three segments: twenty minutes to the presenter, twenty to the panel, and twenty to the general audience.

The first speaker delivered an excellent presentation and then stood ready, as we thought, to listen to the comments of the experts—men and women from fields ranging across many of the categories, such as finance and corporate structure and marketing, that had been addressed in the plan.

Almost immediately it became apparent that he was a backlash listener. Like a television set with a V-chip installed to block violence, he came equipped with an L-chip in his brain to block listening.

Every point raised by the panel was a point to be contested, and contest it he did. His logic was pretty much the same in every instance. "We have already thought of that and here's why it isn't worth my further attention."

Conceding that he probably *had* already thought of it, what was he saying? It seemed he was assuming that if he and his team had simply thought of a problem, it was a problem no more. But if that was it, why seek criticism, why conduct a practice presentation if all the problems were nonproblems?

Let's call that one the intellectual error of the typical backlash listener. There's another kind of error, a breach of courtesy. The panel had devoted hours to studying the business plan and had then freely given its author twenty minutes of uninterrupted air time to present it. The panel was now entitled to its own twenty before the general audience had its turn. But the L-chip speaker, having used up his own air time, proceeded to deny the same privilege to the others. Even when the moderator tactfully pointed this out, he continued to break in with his rebuttals.

The moderator finally literally begged him to listen, but it still didn't work. The reason, and this is obviously a guess, is that his ego was so heavily invested that he saw criticism of his plan as criticism of himself.

With the ground rules now clarified *two or three times* by the moderator everybody expected a more fruitful session when the second presenter took his place at the open end of the U.

What happened was a repeat of the first fiasco. The second speaker too had an implanted L-chip in perfect working order, and he too ignored the pleas of the moderator (while seeming to listen to them). He heard every comment for the sole purpose of finding the issue, then lunged ahead with his rebuttal.

For those who came to take part in an exchange of views on two very interesting startup proposals it was a miserable night. There was no genuine dialogue because dialogue implies two minds engaging. If one of the minds never really engages, you get talk but no interplay of ideas.

Among other attributes, these two presenters lacked empathy. They had no capacity to see a question from the other mind's point of view. I also suspect they were a little short on Subject Mastery. Why else go into such a session with a hair-trigger defense?

At a meeting of the startup group not too long after this double unpleasantness a casually dressed presenter opened with an ironical apology. He was really sorry he needed so little money, and he hoped nobody would care.

Of course we cared right away, in the most positive sense. Next he set his tone—with the psychological equivalent of perfect pitch —by saying, "I'm just a boatbuilder."

All he wanted was a few thousand to set up a boatbuilding business, and he managed somehow to convert his ironical modesty into the "presence" that sends a speaker sailing with the wind at his back. This is the opposite of implying, as so many speakers try to do, that they solve quadratic equations in their head while going to the bathroom.

"I'm just a boatbuilder" somehow translated to a credible statement that he built pretty damned good boats.

All he wanted to do was build more. He delivered a cleanly organized presentation and then listened to the critique of the experts and the queries and comments of the general audience—no attempt to gain fire superiority, no L-chip, no quiveringly sensitive ego—and everybody got what they came for. The experts profited from a stimulating case study, the general audience from a neat presentation and experts' perspective, and the speaker from the presentation practice and critique.

Undoubtedly he and his team had already thought of many of the criticisms, but unless they embodied the whole knowledge of the panel and audience they profited handsomely from their hour in the limelight.

LISTENING AND NERVOUSNESS

Is it a mere coincidence that the boatbuilder was perfectly at ease while the two backlash listeners were tense and driven? *Could there be a connection between real listening and ease of presentation?* Here are three observations, all tending in the same direction.

1. Backlash listeners are hypersensitive to criticism. This suggests a lack of confidence in their own ideas.
2. The lack of confidence suggests that somewhere in their minds they know they aren't fully prepared and their ideas aren't fully developed and tested.
3. Their going ahead with a formal presentation while they are still uncertain about Subject Mastery suggests an underlying confusion about *goals*. Why do it now? To what end?

A speaker who advances a plan prematurely either doesn't see that it's premature (has failed to master the subject) or pushes ahead anyway hoping for applause (so he can skip the trouble of mastering the subject).

And if circumstances compel him to present his plan, make an argument, or participate in a meeting before he's ready—which happens; it's almost a definition of life itself—then he has even less excuse for being a backlash listener.

But is there a connection? Does the person who is *prepared in her own mind* to be a real listener also make an easier presenter?

Experience suggests the answer is yes. It's a matter of the psychology of the speaker.

One reason people get the jitters delivering a standup presentation is that the form of the occasion implies that you, the speaker, are the one with all the answers. All those silent faces, all those expectant eyes turned on you, all those people sitting there while you and you alone stand and speak. There must be a reason for this seemingly unnatural deference, and maybe the reason is that you are Moses coming down from the mountain to reveal Truth to the People.

Most of us, knowing we fall a little short of being Moses, get nervous.

So send an early and clear message that *you are a listener* as well as a speaker. How about: "I'm going to spend the next ten minutes sketching the situation as I see it and offering two recommendations, then I'd be very interested in hearing how *you* see it."

Or: "We've examined this subject from every conceivable angle in previous meetings, and Jim's team has written an excellent action plan. I like the plan but I differ on two pretty important points, and I'd like to suggest a revision. So I hope Jim and his colleagues will give my proposals a good close look before we go over the entire plan point by point."

These aren't wimp openings, they are self-confident ones. If you have to defend your ideas to the death, do it—but don't *start* that way. Be open to the dialogue so you can learn. Use your learning to strengthen your position, if you are justified in so doing. If you have built a good seaworthy ship, it'll ride out the storm and people will know why.

Maybe it's time to stick our heads up and look around. Where are we? We are in the middle of a chapter on *audience*. One way to think of the audience is: *people you want to bond with. Real listening* and *demonstrated listening* are your best bonds to the audience. You cannot bond with him, her, or them unless you first sense them. This means learning who they are by all available means, including the physical senses of sight and hearing.

Yes, listening—rather the *attitude* you have while listening—eases your jitters. That can be very helpful indeed. But let's peel off one more layer. *Why* does it ease the jitters?

Because it helps create a bond. A speaker ought not to be lonely. She or he ought to feel a developing connection with the listeners. This bond, manifested in a willingness to listen on both sides, whether in agreement or disagreement, means you're not alone. You're engaging, you're doing work, you're shifting and weighing and making ideas, in conflict or cooperation with other minds.

THE PARTNERSHIP

The bond won't always lead to something as tangible as a written contract like the one that governs the relationship of venture capitalist and entrepreneur.

At one end of the spectrum it will be just that. But you can succeed as a persuader merely by shifting or shading an attitude. Nobody draws up articles of mutual obligation, and indeed no obligation yet exists, but there's a change in the weather.

If you're arguing for the high price, and a couple of committed low-price partisans leave the meeting with newly opened minds, that's victory. Maybe not the war, but a battle has been won.

The decision of a Hostile to withdraw from active opposition and give your thesis a fair and objective hearing represents a decision on his part to become a real listener. He has in effect said: "I committed too soon. Now I want to expose my mind to the full benefit of your evidence and argument."

Next, suppose you win an agreement in principle. He hasn't said he buys your number, only that you may be right in proposing one somewhere on the high side of the range of numbers under consideration. This too is successful persuasion. You may never bring this guy on board, but you've already moved him twice.

"Moved" him where? To the zone of argument in which he is

likely to see your evidence pretty much as you see it. Now he's more likely to *interpret the evidence* as you do. He's still not a convert but he's *honoring your argument.*

The agreement in principle aligns speaker and audience along the same compass bearing. True, you may not all arrive at the same destination, but you're traveling the same direction, so the chances are good.

Alignments like this represent a meeting of minds, and their utility to the persuader is that they tend to lead to the power-benefit handshake.

Now—right here—the ground starts shifting under our feet. Many readers have already seen that the tidy division between "speaker" or "persuader" on one side and "listener," "audience," or "dialogue partner" on the other cannot be sustained forever. What's happening is that *the audience is moving into a persuasion role,* while the one who started out as the speaker, by engaging in real, demonstrated listening, is moving toward the role of listener.

But, these two are not merely exchanging hats! The hats are starting to multiply. At the start each person had one role; now each is pretty close to playing two at once. Here we have something like an unwritten contract, an agreement among the parties to proceed in good faith.

Let's say I've been trying to persuade ole Billy Bob. He was kind enough to listen, and I sniffed victory as he began to honor my argument with genuine, open-minded attention. Great! says I. I've got this fish as good as netted.

But at just that moment the fish starts talking back, and I find myself thrust into a more complex and challenging role. The drama itself is changing and my role has got to change with it. (But I had better be careful not to change too much.) In order to honor my side of our unspoken compact of mutual respect I have to shut up from time to time, and instead of "speaker" I take the role of "listener." Ole Billy Bob *is now trying to move me.*

This doesn't mean I have lost and he's won. It means we are both winning in that we are now in a dialogue. We're both advancing theses and presumably pursuing goals. These may or may not be antagonistic. But we know this: the clearer my goals the better for me and my team.

What happens next is anybody's guess. If I have crafted my *goals* skillfully and woven my *argument* to give those goals the support they deserve, I still stand an excellent chance of guiding my dialogue partner's energy and power into their service.

At the very least I have achieved the indispensable effect of *bringing the audience to life*. Now we'll see if my goals (which I construe as benefits to me and to him) and my argument can carry us where at the outset I had hoped we'd go. We're now in the exhilarating, sometimes hair-raising part of the persuasion process.

NEGOTIATING VERSUS PERSUADING

There's a whole library out there on negotiation, much of it very useful to the guerrilla, but *negotiation and persuasion are two distinct activities*. To state it with perhaps too much simplicity, negotiation is a phase of persuasion. To bring a listener to the point where he wants to negotiate is itself a persuasion success (depending on where you started). You have to persuade him that there's something here to be negotiated, that you're the one to talk with, and that you're trustworthy.

But this "success" raises a real danger. Are you still a persuader or should you now think of yourself as a negotiator? Are you looking for common interests and an outcome that spreads satisfaction as widely as the situation permits, or are you trying to move the other party toward the power-benefit handshake?

Without venturing farther into the subject of negotiation, we have to observe that the mission of the negotiator and that of the persuader often conflict. Not always but often. And if you define yourself as a negotiator, you may weaken yourself. It may become harder to keep your goals clearly in view and to make sound judgments about adjusting them when it becomes necessary to do so. (If you are not all-powerful, it *will* become necessary.)

But who are you *in your own mind*?

Keep the self-definition of a thought-leader, a persuader, of one who works toward the power-benefit handshake. This is not a selfish role, because the handshake is a pact of mutual benefit. The persuader self-definition does not prevent you from really listening, and it may save you from slipping too far out of a role that adamantly requires you to project the persuader persona described in Chapter 1.

Your conscious idea of who you are is of the utmost importance. Keep it clear.

MOVING TOWARD DIALOGUE

But always move toward dialogue. It may be a ticklish phase of the persuasion process but you'll do all right if you save your essential identity as a persuader while adapting to the more complicated challenge of the dialogue form. You've got to do it; you've got to bring them to life, engage them, involve them in your argument.

A *really inert audience cannot be persuaded of anything.* Bring them to life. Wake them up. Don't be surprised if they start talking.

Persuasion is movement, setting intellectual and emotional energy free. This movement has the formal name of a dialectic, a term that implies an interplay of ideas in which the collision and mixing change at least some of the originals into next-generation relatives. Thus you aren't necessarily a loser if your proposals get modified.

In this book we untangle the elements of the persuasion process and set them out for separate discussion. That's why we have chapters on character, audience, goals, argument, and resistance or pushback. Our point right now is this:

When your radars and sonars start to tell you your audience is getting active and even aggressive—when the earth seems to be shifting under your feet—it doesn't mean you're losing. It means the time has come to play a more complex role and respond to a more complex challenge. This sounds hard but most people welcome it. All you have to do is see how most speakers make the transition from a formal, prepared presentation to the Q&A session.

They relax. Their bodies and faces show relief. They start enjoying themselves. They become fully human and interactive.

This is all to the good if you remember why you are there. You are still a thought-leader, still a persuader, still proposing that others see some aspect of the world as you see it.

"Dialogue" connotes two people talking, but there's a kind of dialogue that doesn't require voiced speech. People interact with speakers and never utter a word. This is dialogue too, in the sense that their ideas mix with and are modified by the speaker's.

And speakers who know how to read the audience will key their presentations to the "data" they sense emanating from the audience. A politician addressing a live audience is a different creature from one talking to a television camera—although even then he or she has usually sensed the audience by means of previous encounters with small groups, staff and press reports, and polls.

The audience thinks, reacts, modifies, and synthesizes from the moment the speaker gains its attention. A speaker who fails to sense these movements and changes will soon drift out of touch. And what you want is precisely *touch*. The power-benefit handshake is touch. It's the listener's decision to dedicate and release his or her power to purposes chosen by the speaker, or by the speaker and listener together in a game of musical hats. (Or it can mean something weaker—for example a subtle shift of attitude that may lead to a true dialogue where none had seemed possible.)

The handshake becomes a reality when both sides expect to reap some benefit someday. Benefits include psychological ones; they may not be monetary or immediate, but they will be realized somehow, some day. The benefit can be as subtle as a belief that by adopting your view I have vindicated my faith in myself as an honest person. I see that your view is more legitimate than my own, and I shift. Having shifted I have done the honest thing and brought my views into more realistic focus. I have moved closer to the truth.

This is persuasion too; this too can lead to action.

Everything we do in audience analysis aims toward the power-benefit handshake. And if we hope to shake hands with the right guy, we have to search the audience pretty carefully to *locate and appreciate the power*. Then with luck we can guide it toward our objectives.

The persuader needs to locate power and coax it out of its cave.

What is power? In political science and philosophy it's an abstraction, one that we all see actualized every day in business. But the powers (plural) that are present in the audience, whether latent or kinetic, are *real and concrete*.

Power and strength are related but not the same. If strength is the ability to control yourself, *power is the ability to control others*. It is the ability to make the right things happen. A speaker who exercises personal strength by *controlling herself* and disciplining her energy—in order to direct it precisely to the place where it'll be most keenly felt—this *strong* person can also become *powerful* by joining her own powers to those she finds in her audience.

How does she find them? By assessing the audience's *knowledge* she searches out the foundations of their power. What they know says something about what they can do. What they can do derives in part from what they know. Sensing, feeling, intuiting their *emotions*, she learns a lot about how they'll interpret and use their knowledge. She breaks the code of their experience. She feels with them.

Developing her *affinity* with them, she sharpens her sense of their style, their wants, needs, and goals. To her knowledge of what they know she adds an emotion-based sense of what they want.

While *listening* to them she may learn things about them and about herself that surprise her. She may see her own goals and perhaps herself as they see her—an invaluable asset to a persuader.

Engaging in a *dialogue* or colloquy with them, she tests her ideas against theirs, exposes both to the hazards of change, and cements a bond with them.

And sorting out the *factions* of the audience, insofar as this is possible, choosing her audience-within-the-audience, she raises the chance that she will craft just the right message and address it in the right tones to the right people. People addressed in this way respond. Their responses teach her even more about them and their agendas. Their agendas declare how they hope to use their power.

Thus the concepts we've been exploring in this chapter—

- Knowledge and emotion in the audience
- Affinity with the audience
- Listening to the audience
- Dialogue with the audience
- Choosing an audience-within-the-audience

help her to see power and place it in its surrounding topography of obstacles and slopes that hinder or accelerate it. They help the speaker gauge the sufficiency or deficiency of the power she finds; to discover and probe its limits and constraints; and to search out its sources. They help her to see *where it has to go* and what it has to do because power unemployed grows rusty. Powerful people know that and it makes them restless, anxious. The persuader's leverage is right there, in *the desire of powerful people to use their power.* They're like horses in good trim and full of oats. They want to see that gate fly open.

This makes the speaker's empathy doubly important. What do these people *want*? A speaker with empathy has a better chance of finding out. Knowing what the audience wants is like knowing how they want to use their power.

Let's say Smythe sets out to persuade the boss to give him a raise. In the middle of his meticulously planned but calmly presented argument the boss cuts him off with, "Look, Smythe, of course you deserve it but so do a couple of others, and the company can't afford raises for everybody. I'll have to take it up with Elaine."

Elaine? Elaine!? Who the hell is she?

It turns out the boss is desperate for capital and has taken on this Elaine figure as a silent partner. Now the old power map is no good. There is no direct line from Smythe's proposal through the boss's assent to Smythe's goal.

The boss is not just an audience any more. Now he's the *primary audience*, the best and maybe the only *channel* to the *secondary audience*, which is another locus of power. Is Smythe foiled? Well if he is, so are we all, because all he's discovered is that the boss's power is constrained.

All power is constrained. As John F. Kennedy once said when somebody suggested he do something as president: That's a great idea. I'll see if I can get the government to go along with it.

POWERS AND THEIR CONSTRAINTS

There are many things the boss can do. He can:

1. Give Smythe the raise.
2. Give him the raise and make him work harder.
3. Deny the raise.
4. Fire him for impudence.

In taking each of these actions the boss seems to be using a different power.

In case 1, giving Smythe the raise, he recognizes merit and reallocates resources. In case 2, giving him the raise and making him work harder, he does both of the above and rewrites a job description. In 3, denying the raise, he leaves his resources untouched but changes something else, namely Smythe's attitude. And in 4, firing Smythe for even daring to ask for the raise, he cuts staff by one and sends a chilling message to the survivors.

Case 3 might seem at first to be an example of powerlessness rather than power, since it could be that the boss denied the raise for lack of funds. But even in that case he has done something, presumably from his point of view *the best thing he could do* in the situation Smythe has forced on him. He has resolved a conflict that he alone has the power to resolve.

But I've asserted that power is always constrained. How is that assertion supported across this range of actions?

To do action 1 the boss had to get his partner's approval. He was constrained by Elaine's power. Likewise for 2, with this added constraint: *something* held him back from giving the raise outright. Maybe the fear of a rush of similar requests, maybe the need to squeeze the last drop of human energy out of a high-paid employee; something. In 3, maybe his partner simply vetoed a raise; maybe the boss decided on his own not to risk seeming inconsistent to Elaine, who he just persuaded to invest in his company; maybe he was afraid she'd say, "Hey, I thought you were keeping an eagle eye on costs!"

In 4 the boss seems to be exhibiting a dread of people who want a fair salary. He has already admitted Smythe deserves a raise, but apparently he can't live with anybody who asks for what he deserves. Is power this arbitrary also constrained? Yes. The head of a business who throws temper tantrums too often will eventually find himself shut off. Orders will drop. People won't return his phone calls. Employees will start sending out their résumés.

The constraints are real. Whether the boss perceives them is a more complicated question, but the chances are that eventually he will.

And even if there were no Elaine and the boss's power appeared to be absolute, that appearance would be deceiving. He would still be constrained. As everyone who has ever administered an organization or even a committee or even a staff picnic knows, the person at the top, the boss, is answerable to his or her *constituencies*.

If you run the staff picnic arbitrarily (that is to say, for your own exclusive pleasure) the picnickers won't enjoy it and your reputation will suffer. Your constituencies are the picnickers and the management, both of whom have a stake in the success of the event.

POWER AND THE CONSTITUENCY

It's becoming clear that if a persuader has to locate power in his audience, he also has to be aware that *powerful people have constituencies* to serve and manage. A constituency is both a source of power and a locus of accountability.

The most familiar example is a member of Congress. Great job; the fate of the nation in your hands and all that. But what do members of Congress actually do all year long? They raise money for campaigns and they agonize over constituent relations. They fly home on the weekends, hold "town hall" meetings and maintain staff in the district, all so they can keep in touch with the constituents and give them the service they expect from an elected representative.

Smythe's boss is similarly empowered and constrained. His most conspicuous constituency is his investors, personified here by Elaine. Without money he goes under; with it he loses his rugged individualism.

But he does not lose his power. He shares it. He tries to keep Elaine happy in order to maintain and strengthen their relationship, which is one of mutual benefit. There's a power-benefit handshake somewhere in their history. Her role is to empower him by lending him money. His is to keep the benefits flowing to her in terms of ROI.

Suppose the boss never needed Elaine. He has his own money and he's as independent as a businessowner can be. He still has constituencies to serve. Customers, employees, suppliers, community. He must maintain good relations with these and more; if he does not, his business ultimately will suffer.

In sensing the persuasion drama *in its entirety* the persuader can only make a useful assessment of the powers he hopes to harness by assessing *the relationships of powerholders with their constituencies.*

How might this work?

Smythe will be well advised to assess how the boss rates him among his peers because Smythe's peer group is one of the boss's constituencies. If the boss irritates them or excites envy and malice by singling Smythe out for a big raise that the peer group feels is undeserved, the boss will soon regret it and so might Smythe.

Smythe's strategy perhaps ought to be to lay less emphasis on how deserving he is and more on differentiating his service to the company from his peers'.

Or take the high-price/low-price example. The decision-maker has to do more than zoom in on the bottom line. He has to balance the competing interests of internal and external constituencies— markets, sales staff, the financial people, the customers, investors, Wall Street, and so on. The whole image of the company is affected by a pricing decision, and DM must feel alternatively empowered and constrained as he runs mentally through the list of people and entities who have a stake in the outcome.

Go ahead, argue for the higher price, but the more you know about DM's relationships with his constituencies the more keenly and accurately you can *feel how he feels* when he ponders his decision.

When your empathy is accurate and far-reaching, you can walk in his shoes. Then one part of your mind (your imaginative empathy), can help the other (the writing, speaking, and composing part), to craft the message you want him to hear.

AGENDAS

There's one more area it will pay us to explore—the *agendas* of the powerholders and their constituencies.

In a splintered audience you'll undoubtedly encounter competing and perhaps incompatible agendas. That's why the audience is splintered. The splinters can often be identified by their agendas. The trouble is that in a large meeting or a large audience assembled for a formal presentation, the agendas can be so numerous and contradictory that they present a hopeless tangle to the speaker.

That's one reason to choose an audience within the audience, so you don't have to worry about a multiplicity of competing interests that are beyond your capacity to please anyway.

The most important agenda is your own, and your job as a persuader is to try to bring others' agendas into near harmony with yours.

We've said enough about listening, empathy, dialogue, and sensing the audience to suggest a general approach to this question of the various agendas a speaker meets in a persuasion drama. They are a given, a found force. They should be accepted and integrated into the speaker's overall, organic *perception of who the audience is.*

When you discern and understand the agendas that drive the listeners you have discovered yet another way to appreciate them and to sense the world as they sense it.

And the use you make of this appreciation is the same as the use you make of other knowledge of the audience. The better you know them the more likely you are to succeed in starting up in their minds the kind of intellectual and emotional processes that lead to assent—assent to your ideas and to you as a person.

TRUST YOUR INSTINCTS

No matter how carefully you approach the job of audience analysis—and even if you have plenty of time, which you seldom will—
there comes a moment when you have to say, "Go!"

You will never know everything that might be useful so when you
feel the go in you, get on with the presentation. Don't let yourself
be hobbled by a never-to-be-satisfied perfectionism. If you keep on
sensing the audience, you will gradually (and perhaps quickly) get
the feel of them and gain confidence that you know, almost instinc-
tively, how to play your role in the unfolding drama.

Keep your antennae tuned. Don't ever shut the audience out.
Once the drama is actually happening, don't even dream of using a
checklist approach to audience analysis. Yes, sensing the audience is
an intellectual activity but it's also an art, something you do with
instincts guided by, but never totally controlled by, your intellect.

This is another place where predetermined systems and algorithms won't work. Just ask yourself some intelligent, penetrating
questions as you move from information-gathering to analysis.

- How much do they know about my proposal?
- Can anybody here take action on it? Who?
- Who out there is likely to be friendly? Why?
- X is distinctly cold, almost hostile. What does that mean?
- If Y agrees with me, will it help or hurt her standing in her peer
  group?

Questions like these lead to others, and as you ponder them you
are likely to find the major concepts of this chapter coming into
play—such concepts as audience power, knowledge and emotions
in the audience, listening, dialogue, sensing the audience, and so
forth. Begin with concrete questions. Move to the concepts, consider them in the abstract, then see what new concrete questions or
answers they generate.

Let your thinking oscillate between the abstract and the concrete, between the concepts and your own questions and answers
about this specific audience. The best instincts are those that are
informed, trained, and sharpened by conscious intellectual work

such as the concepts require. And the best intellectual work is the kind that is guided and inspired by your instincts as a human being living among other human beings.

Do as much of this work as you feel is helpful before you speak. When you start speaking, abandon all formal analysis. You have reached Go. But keep the channel open, because in the active sensing of your audience there is no such word as Stop.

3

Goals and Gremlins —
How Vague Desire Can
Screw Up the Works

There's a hoary old truth of war and politics that "action is guided by those who know what they want." Like a lot of other hoary old truths, this one is perhaps more complicated than it sounds. Certainly in business "knowing what you want" isn't the same as carving a clear and achievable *goal* out of a landscape you choose to define as an *opportunity*.

The startup group had assembled to hear the presentation of a business plan by a woman who wanted to go into the dude ranch business.

She was a good presenter. She spoke clearly, in a voice all could hear. She knew the difference between opinion and argument, and she exhibited a good command of each individual aspect of her plan.

But as she went deeper into her allotted time some of her listeners began to worry. Was she really *there* as a person? Did the plan hang together?

After about ten minutes a listener could have identified one problem in presentation and another in content. The first was an apparent failure to project a *persuasive persona*. She was an excellent speaker but technique alone is never enough.

The second was a failure of some kind in the plan itself. Perhaps only a very wise head could have said what it was—and fortunately there was just such a sage among us that night.

He was a developer with prior experience as a business consultant. He spoke for about two minutes and in those 120 seconds he pulled three separate businesses out of the plan. She was: 1) in the tourism business, 2) in the land speculation business, and 3) in the business of buying, improving, and reselling dude ranches.

It was one of those pivotal moments when virtually everybody in a room realigns his or her thinking. The critic leaned forward and said with all kindness and all candor, "You don't seem to be sure what business you're in."

All three ideas were struggling for full expression in the plan and none was capable of shaping it into a coherent whole. This explained both problems—that something felt wrong in the plan *and* the presenter.

If the critic was right, the woman was presenting too soon. She had gone public with her plan before she fully understood it herself. More specifically, she had mistaken her desire to live in a certain place and in a certain way, to make a living in the Rockies, to ride and teach riding and so forth—had mistaken this dream for a program. A dream or desire is a source of energy, courage, and hope. But it is not a program, and it can deceive the dreamer as well as inspire her.

The creative businessperson ought to be inspired by her or his dream but not intoxicated. You start with a dream; you follow through with a *program*. And a program embodies goals and usually series of goals, together with the plan and the means to carry it out.

And if the critic was right, then the speaker's failure to project a convincing persona was explained too. A persuader's goals are an integral part of who she is. If her goals are not fully developed, she will seem unclear to her audience, at best, and unprepared at worst. She has to master her subject, and she simply can't do it if she's not sure what business she's in.

This doesn't mean a speaker must state one goal and one only; and it doesn't mean this entrepreneur couldn't have devised a business plan combining all three of the ideas identified by her critic. But if she did that, her plan would have to support it. "This is a business with three revenue streams deriving from activities A, B, and C. Here's how my financials support all three. Here's my team, with talents spread over all three areas. Here's how I expect the synergies to work . . ."

But there was nothing like that because her plan projected a desire without a program to sustain it. Everyone in that room admired the excellent work that had gone into the separate parts of the plan, and her courage in plunging into it; but hard work and courage couldn't make up for what the plan lacked. And what it lacked was exactly what the critic was pointing to: a coherent and integrated set of goals against which to test everything else.

Desires are subjective, but goals have to be convincing objectively. A goal in business has to pass a hard test. It has to be convincing even to those who do not necessarily share the dream and feel the passion, such as investors.

There is a kind of rigorous, disciplined work that looks at the dream from the outside, examines the desire *dispassionately*, and tests it for soundness in an uncaring world—for *realism*. Having passed this test, the desire still has to be translated into a business program that makes it a reality. Desire and program merge to form that living thing called a business.

But untested, undisciplined desire can be a gremlin, an unseen bug in the works. How does it do its mischief? By making you think you "know what you want" when all you really know is what you wish.

In this chapter we'll make it our business to examine goals to see what they're made of; to distinguish *action goals* from *persuasion goals*; and to show how the basic persuasion goals serve a program of action.

THE RIGHT QUESTION

What the dude ranch entrepreneur needed, and what we all need, is a well-developed ability to ask ourselves the right questions. There is an absolutely basic, essential question about goals: "*What do you think you're doing?*"

Not: What *are* you doing? What do you *think* you're doing?

At the macro level corporations keep this question before their employees' eyes by publishing mission statements or statements about "corporate vision."

"We will strive to be the leader in providing X and Y services to individuals and businesses. We will relentlessly pursue new ideas and strategies to enable our clients to achieve their goals."

Let's call this the macro level because such statements are too general to guide an employee through the typical working day. They do, however, serve to engender an attitude in the employee and to represent the company's aspirations to other constituencies such as customers, suppliers, and shareholders.

At their best, mission statements can provide a pair of basic concepts: what *kind of business* you're in; what *kind of person* you need to be in order to succeed in that business.

From General Motors right down to a solo consultant doing business out of his home, everybody needs clarity on these two concepts. By themselves they do not generate goals, and they are perhaps too vague to help somebody like the dude ranch entrepreneur. But they do something that is quite indispensable.

Once they are pondered, tested, clarified, and accepted they serve to indicate a general direction in which to proceed and a general way of working. Without this, setting goals is logically impossible. We need a) a global concept of what we're doing and b) a sense of who we are while doing it. That's why failure is so instructive; it forces us back to a rigorous reexamination of the two basic concepts.

But a concept, however necessary, is not a goal. What you're supposed to get from both concepts and goals is a form of self-guidance. "If I am a certain kind of person working in a certain kind of enterprise, I will behave like this and not like that."

The difference between general concepts of the kind to be found in a "corporate vision" and goals is that goals offer surer guidance. Goals guide and drive effort from day to day and hour to hour. It is goals that answer that persistent question still sounding in our ears: "What do you think you're doing?"

It appears that we need something sharper and harder than, "I'm relentlessly striving to make my company the national leader in X." What we need is guidance *within* the two basic concepts. We need to know what to do this year, this month, this week, *today*, and right now.

A GOAL IS A WAY STATION, NOT A DESTINATION

If a goal is to be useful, it has to be someplace you pass through. *A goal is not the end of the line.* Having reached it you don't say, "Well here we are, the national leader and our clients have met all their goals, so I guess we shoot ourselves."

It's true that dictionaries almost always speak of a goal as the *end*—the end toward which you direct your effort, hope, and ambition. But in the real world it isn't that way. Sure, a goal is something you aim at, but the moment you reach this "end" you find no resting place. This is true in politics, diplomacy, military operations, baseball, and business, and equally true in "lifestyle" ambitions as well, since nothing achieved ever turns out exactly as expected. And a lifestyle, like a business or a military operation, is an organic blending of many elements, one of which is growth (or its opposite).

So let's take this as a sort of revelation: a goal—no matter what the dictionaries say—is not an "end," not in the sense of a stoppage or resting place. It is indeed something we aim at, and there the dictionaries are right. "Aim" implies design; and this is the key to goal-setting in the business life. A goal is an aim, the aim specifically of a *design*, plan, or process. To get there you lay out a course of action. It's not a mere desire, not a dream, even though dreams are dynamos. It's a planned outcome depending for its success on somebody making it happen "by design."

So let's turn the dictionary definition on its head. Let's look at a goal not as an end but a means, not as the place you land but as a springboard, not as a thing to be valued for its own sake but as an instrument for achieving something else.

Since an instrument is something you make use of to accomplish something else, there should be ways to tell whether it's going to work. It is after all something practical, and if it's not practical, it's not worth aiming at. How do you tell if some goal you have in mind, some aim, really will turn out to be a springboard and not a swamp?

If you could figure out what you might do today that would be useful tomorrow—something that would help you to *keep striving* in what your concepts tell you is *the right direction*—then you could safely say to yourself, "This thing I want to do today *is a goal*. And the reason I call it a goal is that it will help me move on to some other achievement—something I do by design—that will in turn help me move forward again."

Businesspeople have to devise goals every day, and the problem is especially acute for guerrillas because they do the devising themselves. They seldom *take* direction; they *choose* directions.

One such guerrilla—an entrepreneur who has faced extraordinarily complex challenges and still faces them—is Chris Stevens, marketing and sales boss for a six-person startup.

As Stevens explained it, his company, Keurig, Inc., set itself the corporate goal of placing quality, brewed-by-the-cup coffee in offices. All offices have coffee but few serve anything to equal the upscale brews that more and more drinkers are hooked on. Keurig saw this as a great opportunity to reach a huge, underserved market.

All six people on the Keurig team are essential but the most conspicuous of the make-or-break roles is Stevens's marketing task. If the coffee was terrific, the brewing machines reliable, and the distributors efficient, it still wouldn't make any difference if Stevens couldn't pry open a niche. How did he propose to do it?

First, by remembering the lessons of his experience.

After graduating from Notre Dame he played one year of pro basketball then went to work as a bag-toting salesman for Procter & Gamble. He wore out his shoes in Chicago, Pittsburgh, and Detroit before being assigned to corporate headquarters in Cincinnati, where he worked in a sales merchandising division. His last job at P&G was district sales manager for New England ($60 million in sales a year).

He moved to Anheuser-Busch as president and general manager of the company-owned distributor in Boston, then to a job as division manager for thirty independent wholesalers in New England ($600 million a year). Stevens left the world of the big corporations, did some consulting, and took over as executive vice president of a spirit, wine, and beer distributor before finally making the leap to an equity stake in the coffee startup.

What do you learn in twenty-plus years doing this kind of work?

A lot, but one of his themes really stands out. It's simple but revealing. He sees business *as a process.*

To Chris Stevens business, or some "event" in business, such as a sale, is not really an event in the sense of a single, self-contained action. It is part of a process, *a series of subordinate and connected events,* one leading to another. Events happen. Processes continue. Therefore Stevens works by setting a series of graduated goals. It's like jumping from rock to rock as you cross a stream. You don't try to jump clear across in one desperate leap even if you've got the legs of a pro basketball player.

You measure the distance with a careful eye and try to *achieve what's achievable.* Having done this you try to achieve something else.

And here he harked back to his P&G training. He quoted the company's SMAC mnemonic for testing the validity and usefulness of goals. They must be: *specific, measurable, achievable,* and *compatible.* And he added a fifth of his own: they must serve the business plan in some *essential* way.

This is how Stevens guides himself through days and weeks when he could be flailing around doing just about anything. Say an idea pops into his head—he wonders if he should establish a Beta site at Company X, a test site operating in the real world. Sounds pretty good, but suppose he already has three Beta sites running. How does he decide whether to assign a portion of his time and energy to establishing a fourth?

He tentatively defines the fourth site as a goal and tests it against his five criteria. Is this goal

- Specific
- Measurable
- Achievable
- Compatible
- Essential

If it's *specific* he can see the job clearly and draw boundaries around it. It doesn't mean opening some massive interface with Company X or trying to network the whole place. It means running a test operation there and that's all it means.

And if it's *measurable,* then Stevens can somehow sense its impact, maybe with numbers, maybe by feel. But somehow or other the Beta site at this particular company has to yield knowledge he can use in evaluating, say, customer reaction to the taste of the coffee.

Does what he learns merely duplicate what he's learning at the other sites? If so, is that O.K.? Does he need confirmation of older impressions? If not, what will he learn at the new site? Will he somehow be able to tell when enough is enough?

If it's *achievable*, he can do it without devoting more time to it than it's worth. If he has to make twenty visits and a hundred phone calls, it may be achievable in some abstract way but, practically speaking, he'll forget it. He'll look for some other way to spend his time.

If it's *compatible*, it will fit into his business plan—for example, by replicating the kind of market he's interested in. And the coffee will *blend into* the atmosphere at Company X. He wouldn't set up a Beta site for upscale coffee in a quick-stop oil-change shop: not the right market; the data wouldn't be relevant.

And if it's *essential*, it will somehow advance the business plan. It will show weaknesses, for example, in the brewing machines. Maybe they require too much maintenance. Maybe the water temperature needs adjusting. Or maybe the machines pass all tests and the plan is served by being validated under field conditions. It's essential to know if you're wrong but equally essential and somewhat more pleasant to know when you're right.

Stevens's use of "essential" is pretty elastic. It means a goal you had better pursue or you might regret it later. This standard is softer than the dire necessity the word "essential" implies.

THE GOAL AS A SPRINGBOARD

Now we're moving beyond Stevens's criteria to the next logical one, which is "bounce."

You do the SMAC test, you add Stevens's criterion of essentiality; now add the test of whether the goal yields more energy than it consumes. Is it a swamp or a springboard? Does it have *bounce*?

Suppose Stevens decides the goal is worth it. He works like a dog and starts a Beta site at Company X. We'll cheer his effort if we observe that hitting this goal gave him a bounce of some kind. What are the possibilities?

The site can reveal surprising data, reactions to the coffee that he didn't expect. It's too bitter, too weak, too smoky, too nutty. He investigates and finds—let's suppose—that the coffee supplier has changed something without consulting him. The site has done a good thing, and Stevens bounces to a new goal with the energy of new knowledge.

Suppose they love him at Company X. They can't get enough of his coffee. He's the guy who brings terrific coffee at reasonable prices and they're begging him to draw up a contract even before he's ready to move to market. So he's confirmed in his optimism and can go ahead even more confidently than before. This is a bounce. He's sweeping the horizon for new goals.

Or, a few employees of X love the coffee but most stay away. What's wrong? Is this market softer than he thought? Is X different from his other sites in ways he didn't suspect? This bounces him too—he'd better find out what's going on. Maybe this "finding out" is his next goal. In these conditions the Beta site does begin to look like a springboard.

It looks like a goal that was specific, measurable (at least roughly), achievable, and compatible, plus, in Stevens's view, essential. And it gave him a bounce well worth his investment.

It was the kind of goal whose achievement gives you a shot of energy toward some other goal or goals which, if you don't get dizzy, you need to evaluate in the same way and try to get your next bounce.

There may be some grand epistemological system for *inventing* goals but I doubt it'd be of much help. Inventing goals is a process much closer to instinct than is the separate activity of evaluating them. Goals pop up in your mind and shout for attention. There's no point in asking: "Where did *you* come from?" They come from your creative intellect; from your dreaming, desiring, hoping; and from playful emotions working on that intellect to help it do its job.

Or in another common scenario goals come out of conferences

and brainstorming sessions. Wherever they come from, they all require objective and rigorous testing.

So art and instinct have their roles to play; but so does the systematic testing of the goals that crowd in on you, whether originating in your mind or coming at you from external origins, including the boss. What we've seen here is Stevens's take on the P&G formula blended into our take on Stevens. *SMAC + Essentiality + Bounce.*

By the way, I don't mean to imply that a working day or a project consists of a single chain of neatly connecting goals. Obviously it's more complicated. But the point about the springboard is that if a goal, once achieved, has consumed more energy than it yields, maybe it was a mistake to pursue it. You've got a letdown instead of a bounce.

Before we leave Stevens let's watch him doing exactly what that I-banker we watched a while ago failed so conspicuously to do.

What he did was present a heap of moderately interesting information while missing a golden opportunity to impress an elite audience with the high quality of his firm's people. In the language of our first chapter, he failed to exploit an opportunity to engender trust and respect.

To judge by his actions, his goal was simply and boringly to present information, that is, to "give a speech." This "goal" had no bounce to it. When he sat down, nothing had happened—there was nothing else to do *but* sit down.

In a similar situation Chris Stevens set himself a goal with bounce: to show an important audience that there was something out of the ordinary about the people working the Keurig startup.

It was possible to deduce that this was his goal while he was holding that audience in the palm of his hand. His *assignment* was to critique an entrepreneur's case presentation. It was a case about a startup microbrewer (beer, not coffee). There were three critics, and the other two did the job with intelligence and sagacity—and some listeners felt that at least one of the other critics offered more content than Stevens did. But the speaker who stood out that night, and the one who'll be remembered both for dazzling showmanship and excellence of content, was Stevens.

He started in a way that's unaccountably rare among business speakers. He got off his rear and *moved*.

Instead of speaking from the critics' table, which was across the proscenium from the presenter's lectern, he went straight to the lectern—showing his body, in our terminology—and proceeded to play an audiotape of his own impersonation of Walter Cronkite broadcasting the news that a distinguished crowd had gathered that night to analyze a brewing business. The Cronkite parody was neither extraordinarily good nor bad. It was O.K., and it was Stevens's own invention: nothing canned or predictable about it. Then he slapped a stack of overheads down by the machine—but nobody groaned. We already knew that the last thing this guy would ever do was bore us with a bunch of visuals.

He took off his coat. More body, more "presence," more immediacy. A suit coat can stand between you and your audience. It can say, "I'm just like everybody else, hiding my body cause it's so blah." Take the damn thing off, and whatever else you may do, at least you cancel that deadening message.

His visuals—which he *did not talk to*—were informative but not extraordinary; but they did their job by helping to shape his critique, and to etch his main points into the consciousness, which is all visuals can ever do. He raced through his critique (too fast—his only major failing as a presenter) and he livened it all with humor and *goodwill*—another trait that too many presenters seem to forget about. He was trying to be useful to the brewing entrepreneur but something else was going on too.

He sat down, having run over his time by a minute or two (no big deal), and the audience boomed out its approval. Not because his presentation technique was perfect, although it was very good; not because his content was markedly better than what the other two critics offered (they hadn't yet spoken), although his content was organized, substantive, and probably helpful to the entrepreneur. No—they loved him for the verve, originality, and daring of his performance.

Probably 90 percent of the people in that audience had given presentations and knew how hard it can be. *This is typical of business audiences. Having tried it themselves, they are primed to appreciate something bold that justifies the boldness.*

Feeling that way about it myself, I sought him out and asked what he had been trying to do that night. Did he have a clear goal? He answered in two parts: 1) he wanted to do the assigned job and do it well—that is, to help the entrepreneur through informed criticism of his operation; and 2) he wanted to make a personal impression.

He went there as the representative of his company. Meaning he had clearly defined his "psychology of the speaker." He knew who he was from the moment he stepped to the microphone. His goal was a country mile from the dead-end idea of "conveying information." What he wanted to do was show that this obscure little startup that hardly anybody in the audience had even heard of was a first-class outfit.

There are three lessons here.

1. *Prepare, prepare, prepare.* Stevens had studied the entrepreneur's business, visited the brewery, and given careful thought to marketing and sales issues. He never had to skate or fake it. If you take on a job like that and don't deliver, everybody in the room knows it.
2. *Show your passion.* People want to do business with people who have passion. There are various ways to communicate it, but one of the best is to throw yourself into your presentation and thereby show how much you value the opportunity and respect the audience.
3. *Entertainment enhances learning. Boredom kills it.* Stimulate the audience with humor and "presence" and they'll notice, assimilate, and retain twice as much.

For example Stevens said at the very start of his presentation, addressing the entrepreneur, not the general audience: "These critiques can be pretty rough. You're about to find that out." In other words he started with an entertaining sentence—not Steve Martin, but a ripple of laughter went through the audience and Stevens had set a tone for what he planned to do later.

It wasn't the content that was remarkable; it was the presenter, who combined a dash of charisma with irony, goodwill, wit, and "presence."

As a goal, his aim of "representing his company" meets the four P&G criteria, the Stevens "essential" criterion (if by essential you don't mean "dire necessity" but rather exploiting the present occasion to advance the business plan), and it meets our "bounce" criterion too. It bounces him ahead by giving his firm a sparkling image among three hundred fifty of the most involved and energetic businesspeople in town, who were, moreover, there because of their interest in the retail beverage industry.

Could he give a convincing answer to the basic goal question, "What do you think you're doing?" Sure he could.

SYMBIOSIS: PERSUASION GOALS AND ACTION GOALS

A pitcher goes into his windup. He convinces the batter and, incidentally, the hostile runner on first that he's pitching to the plate. These are developments, processes he has encouraged *in the minds* of the batter and base runner. He wheels and throws to first, catches the runner off base, and has the pleasure of watching the first baseman tag him out. This is something the pitcher caused *in the world*.

This is a typical sequence. Things happen in the world when some necessary preliminary condition has been achieved in somebody's mind.

In the preceding pages Chris Stevens did two things. He impressed an audience—etched *in their minds* a positive image of himself and his company. And he set up a Beta site *in the world* (the physical world and the world of business).

When you set out to change what's going on in somebody's mind, you are pursuing a *persuasion goal*. When you set out to change the way they act, you are pursuing an *action goal*.

Our examples taken from Stevens's career are not related to one another but a little imagination would show how they could be. Say an executive from Company X is in the audience at his presentation and comes up to shake his hand. The two begin talking about what

Stevens is doing. Stevens might mention that he's looking for Beta sites. The executive might say, "Why not us? I'm with Company X."

Having highlighted the difference between action goals and persuasion goals we should add this—it's virtually impossible to disentangle them. Strong persuasion skills develop your ability to cause and guide action. Effective action enhances your reputation and gives you a more potent character as a persuader. This helps you influence other minds, which leads to more effective action.

You can also spiral downward. A single misstep can sometimes destroy your credibility, and thereafter people simply turn you off. No matter if you have a good argument, they aren't listening anymore.

The two kinds of goals are alike in another respect. They respond to the same tests. You can use SMAC + Essentiality + Bounce on both kinds. And in both the purpose is the same, to help you answer the basic goal question: what do you think you're doing?

The chief virtues of this question are that it helps you guide present action and look forward to future consequences. Philosophers, theologians, and jurists have been insisting for centuries that we humans intend the consequences of our actions. To intend to do something is the same morally as intending its foreseeable consequences. Of course not all consequences are predictable or intended but most are, which is why we hold ourselves responsible for what we do, or argue so vehemently that we are *not* responsible.

Recognizing then that persuasion and action are mutually reinforcing (and that this is a book about persuasion) we want now to see how some common persuasion goals fit into a program of action.

AUDIENCE-SPECIFIC GOALS

A persuasion opportunity is a chance to cause a certain *limited effect* on a certain audience.

Big Customer is coming to town. Your boss planned to meet him at the airport but sends you at the last minute. You've got a half-hour alone in the car with BC. What do you do?

Or Company Q is descending into chaos. The CEO died six months ago and his son is living proof of Ataturk's dictum that great men should father no sons. You're invited to meet with the board. What do you do?

Maybe you're a broker with a nervous Nellie client whose nightmares keep telling him it's 1987 all over again. You see a rising market. He's quivering on the other end of your phone line. What do you do?

In these and a hundred other scenarios the persuader chooses from a wide array of fairly specific goals that are appropriate to the actual drama. Specific, appropriate, but most of all *limited*.

Your long-term goal is always the power-benefit handshake in one of its many forms, and you achieve it when the other mind moves into harmony with yours. But minds cannot be forced into motion. They can only be moved by being *shown*, and they need to see something that appeals to the intellect or emotions. Having seen it, *they move themselves.*

That's why skilled persuaders will search each persuasion opportunity for its potential and, equally important, will recognize where the potential ends. The biggest mistake a business persuader can make is moving in for the quick kill. A skilled persuader sets *graduated* persuasion goals while keeping the long-term goal clearly in view. She or he seeks to do in each stage of the process *that which can be done* and no more.

Of course you recognize that when the listener is ready for the handshake, you hold out your hand—but the handshake is the culmination of the persuasion process, not the process itself.

Thinkers move toward decisions, or toward new attitudes, in stages, on the basis of new information or insights. Let's call that number 1. Thinkers move in stages.

And number 2 is that they tend to consolidate their thinking at each new stage. They pause to become accustomed to the new state of mind. A skilled persuader tries to design her persuasion in such a way as to leave intervals for this consolidation.

Taking 1 and 2 into account, it would be unwise to jump into the car with Big Customer, slam the door, and sing out: "Hey BC! What do you say we triple your order?"

BC would think you were kidding. After all, he doesn't even

know who you are. The job is to identify persuasion goals that you can achieve and that stand a chance of moving BC's mind in the right direction.

In the next few minutes we'll look at some basic persuasion goals. The ones you choose will depend on the audience and the opportunity, and on how they fit into your business.

You can apply SMAC + Essentiality + Bounce in choosing your persuasion goals. As these formalized tests become habitual they'll also become unconscious, automatic, and quick. Conscious analysis will give way to trained instinct. Here are the goals.

Present Yourself

We said enough about self-presentation in Chapter 1, but it deserves to be placed here at the top of the list, and for the very same reasons we gave it such thorough treatment earlier. Your persona is your most powerful asset. It is also the best asset your company has in the one-scene drama of your ride from the airport with BC. Maybe that's why the boss sent you.

Self-presentation is the threshold goal. It's the beginning.

Instill an Attitude

Once you accept a word of caution about moving in for a quick kill, and you ponder numbers 1 and 2 above, you readily see that instilling or encouraging an attitude in the listener can be a step forward.

Sheila Sinclair, who worked as a fundraiser for a university before moving on to a rainmaker's job for asset-management firms on Wall Street, tells a story about a potential donor to the university where she used to work. She had been in contact with him over a long period and had observed the signs of a man about to decide on a major gift. Then his son was rejected by the school, and worse yet, the rejection came after the admissions office had made some equivocal statements that seemed to imply the young man might be admitted after all.

In her talks with the father Sinclair showed her empathy (quite naturally; she has it in abundance) and let him "talk it out." When he talked about how the admissions office seemed to have acted inappropriately, Sinclair decided it was time to utter her key response.

"It wouldn't matter so much to you if you didn't care so much about the school." This was her attempt—successful, as it turned out—to reawaken his affection for his old school.

The listener's *attitude* governs the way he or she interprets the so-called fact. Facts are never neutral. Even a thermometer reading can be frigid or bracing, depending on your attitude.

Work on the Relationship

In its early stages a persuasion task is often a nurturing of relationships. This phase is often lacking in "content" of the kind we think of as text, as facts, evidence, premises, and conclusions. But it's not wasted labor, it's more like laying the groundwork for later presentation of facts and so forth.

Since so much depends on the character of the persuader, since you persuade largely through the persona you project, it follows that the relationship is critical. It is the medium through which people connect. The relationship you develop with the audience or dialogue partner is the atmosphere you both breathe. Make it a healthy one.

Sinclair said she spends a huge amount of her time researching her dialogue partners and cultivating an interest in the subjects that interest them. There's nothing phony about this. All the parties know exactly what's going on—that Sinclair wants to awaken in them an interest in a certain fund or syndication.

The question is, are they going to enjoy this or not? And beyond that lies another, will the relationship flourish?

If the relationship is good, the chance of its being put to business use is good. If not, it will wither. Everybody understands this from the start, and each party is constantly "sensing" the other. And both or all parties—not just the persuader—seek to engender respect and trust. It's human nature.

To take Steve Ricci's triad and place it in a different context: concept and deal are not enough. People matter too.

Emphasize Affinity

Within the context of the relationship it pays to develop affinity where it is legitimate and possible to do so.

We need not repeat what we've said about affinity. We'll add only that, like friendship, it is a thing of value in itself, something to be prized for its own sake. It can be useful in a persuasion attempt—but the persuader must always ask herself or himself: What use of affinity is consistent with the integrity of the person I want to be?

If a value is turned into a mere asset, somebody is not thinking clearly; somebody is risking his integrity by pawning his sincerity.

Establish a Vocabulary

Sometimes a word or phrase will have the effect of organizing a discussion around a new or altered theme. Take the innocuous phrase "risk-averse."

It takes the self-evident concept that investing is risky business and puts it in clear view for all to see. Whoever uses the term shows that he or she is not hiding behind some fantastic claim that this or that investment is a sure thing.

"So-and-So's a risk-averse investor." It carries neither praise nor blame (unless the speaker puts a spin on it). It makes a statement about the investor's attitude.

The phrase also implies that there is a whole range of risk—from warm and cuddly to suicidal—and that the issue for the potential investor is not so much whether to invest but *where* to invest along that spectrum.

The term also implies that the speaker is quite ready to respect a very conservative attitude. "You don't like these put options? O.K., we'll look for something a little less risky."

Or take "core business," another term with power to shape a conversation.

On your ride in from the airport Big Customer asks if your company sells mall space on the Internet. You can say, "Uh-huh" or you can say, "Yes, that's part of our core business."

You thereby imply that you not only do it but do it well and regularly. You have also given him a tantalizing hint about your firm. He's been buying certain services and now he hears that another service is part of your "core business." His impulse is to follow up on the hint and find out what else you offer. Your word "core" implies both a center and a periphery. What's going on in both areas?

Some terms have an honorific or romantic glow—entrepreneur, inventor, pro bono, volunteer, startup, angel, case team leader. Still others carry the whiff of decay or incompetency—unfocused, spread too thin, jargon, boring, self-indulgent.

Name the Pattern

Much dialogue and discussion is guided by pattern recognition. People talking about patterns they don't recognize as such usually sound confused and wobbly. The one who recognizes the pattern first gains an advantage. She stakes her claim by introducing a term that names the pattern, and the others, like it or not, have to pick up the term, in effect borrowing her dictionary. Their use of her term reflects credit on the originator, and the more sharply the talk focuses on the pattern the more credit she gets for starting the ball rolling.

Nobody is derided so mercilessly as an MBA candidate who tries to take credit for discovering a pattern that some other person named five minutes before.

Let's click on the critique of the dude ranch business plan. We've already seen how one astute critic opened everybody's eyes. He did so precisely by searching for a pattern (in the shape of a viable business description) and concluding that none existed. Hence his declaration that the presenter didn't seem to know what business she was in.

But it's easy to imagine a parallel case in which a critic examined a business plan and analyzed it like this:

"I'm afraid I don't see a description here of a viable business. Obviously that's a problem if you're trying to attract venture capital.

"But I do see something else, namely a commitment to a lifestyle. All right then, let's look at this as the early stage of a plan to create a *lifestyle business*. If that's what you're doing, two things follow. First, scale back your thinking to something more modest. Second, forget about venture capital. Why give up equity? Clarify your business idea as a lifestyle business, then start talking to bankers about an ordinary commercial loan."

Everything this critic has said, every syllable, is implied in his pattern-name: "lifestyle business." When you recognize a pattern, especially when you see it first *and name it*, you give shape and coherence to that phase of the drama. This is what thought-leaders do. Being recognized as a thought-leader is a potent asset.

The goal of introducing a vocabulary is an interim goal on the road to the centrally important goal of engendering respect and trust.

Set the Agenda

By naming the pattern you position yourself to set the agenda. When you succeed at this, you control the flow of thought at least for a while. It becomes necessary for other thinkers and speakers to settle certain questions, some of which they might prefer to by-pass. "Setting the agenda" puts those questions squarely in the path ahead.

You're a member of a team developing an outsourcing plan. Unions in your city are charging companies like yours with dumping American workers into near-poverty by exploiting the labor of desperate third-world workers whom you pay in the coin of slavery — fifty or sixty cents an hour.

Some on your team are sympathetic to these views, and there are dilemmas here that may be insoluble. But you can provide a framework for the team's thinking by laying down a challenge: "Who in this room believes we can isolate the U.S. economy from the rest of the world?"

The agenda is now set for the next phase of the discussion. Obviously we are not an economic island, so an agenda unscrolls with several tough questions, especially: what does the interdependence of economies imply about outsourcing to the cheapest labor market?

An agenda is not an answer, but it will throw questions on the screen in a kind of hierarchy, loading some with value and unloading others. The agenda that flows from this question is clearly tilted toward cheap outsourcing.

The question is one of pattern. It assumes the validity of the main elements of what has come to be called the global economy, and it challenges dissenters to refute those assumptions.

Thus by organizing the talk within a pattern—by sending the message, "We live in the global economy and break its rules at our peril"—the questioner not only sets the agenda for the next phase but also puts the burden of the argument on the dissenters. In fact the very term "dissenters" enthrones a thesis from which the dissenter dissents.

Suppose now you're a dissenter, one of those more concerned with American workers slipping than with fitting us into the global economy. How do you respond to this agenda-setting question?

Obviously you try to seize control of the agenda yourself, in such a way as to focus on the present losses of American families rather than on grand theories of international trade.

The key point is that you don't try to answer the other guy's question in any serious way. To do so is to commit the discussion to the whole agenda that unscrolls from it.

You can brush it off—"Sure, sure, we all know the economies of the world are interrelated, but that's not the point."

And this is perfectly legitimate. You're not denying it's *a* point; you're denying it's *the* point. He might say: "Hey there, are you afraid to answer my question? Let's have a little intellectual fortitude here!"

But of course he's bluffing. He has not established a sovereign right to construct the agenda; all he's done is *claim* that right. Looking closer at what he's done we see that he has not proved anything, has not even *argued* anything. All he has done is ask a provocative question. His question unscrolls a list of agenda items that any honest attempt to deal with the question would have to face.

But that's exactly what's at issue: *Must we start with his question?* In other words, when somebody tries to seize the initiative in establishing the agenda, look in his thinking for the fallacy of "begging the question."

In this case the questioner wants us to yield to his claim that we have to start where he says we have to start. O.K., counter him.

You can flat-out refuse the challenge. "Maybe that's *your* question, Harold. I hope you find the answer. But we live in this city and do business here. The people here are our people, and the company is supposed to be committed to the welfare of this town. Let's fit *that* into our outsourcing policy."

This too sets an agenda. Who wins the tussle depends on all the forces in the drama including the quickness, boldness, and *character* of the players.

Two other ways to set the agenda—by introducing "facts with legs" *(premises)* and by structuring your idea as a *thesis*—will be taken up in the next chapter.

Meanwhile let's look at a few more basic persuasion goals.

Open a Channel; Empower an Advocate

If you see that the real power is located elsewhere, outside your audience, you may be talking to the wrong people. But before you reach that conclusion, look for power's handmaiden: *influence*.

A common and unmistakable case is the loan officer who cannot grant your loan on his own authority but has plenty of pull with those who can.

The loan committee won't see you; this man is your only *channel* to the powerholders, so strive to make him your *advocate* as well. Treat him as if he were the decision-maker. Try to cover the whole triad and to gain his respect and trust, but *go a little beyond this*, for the simple reason that he can't bottle your charisma and uncork it in the committee room.

Give him something to carry—written material and graphics that he can pass out at the committee meeting. If there's a business plan, be sure he has enough copies. If not, furnish him your résumé, an executive summary of your project, and simple financials.

Salt your conversation with *memorable phrases and sentences* to crystallize his thinking. With luck he'll repeat one or two to the committee. For example:

"This isn't going to be an ordinary restaurant; it's a bistro and wine bar."

"We'll serve the best French food in town to people who can appreciate it."

"Every wine on our list will be available by the glass."

"We'll bake our own bread, and we have hired just the woman to do it, Mme. Lulu from Chez Jacques."

Give him props—a picture of the site, a loaf of fresh bread, a dessert tray, a menu, a photo postcard of the chef and host. Exhibits, props, and quotes will lend zip and imagery to his presentation. Hit the verbals with all your skill because they shape his thinking and may shape the committee's too.

But the key to successful *relay communication* (which we'll examine in the chapter on pushback) is still respect and trust. If you have really brought him on board as your advocate, those feelings will accompany him into the committee room and bounce off the walls.

Rally the Troops; Instill Motivation

We've already seen how one senior executive, John Pope of Reader's Digest, motivates his teams, and the importance he attaches to it. Pope aims, in our terminology, to *instill an attitude.*

Instilling an attitude, rallying the troops, and instilling motivation are goals that stretch along a continuum. All require the same activity by the persuader and all lead in the same direction.

We call it "rallying the troops" when you are able to carry the attitude to a level of commitment in which the troops start to believe intensely in the goals of the project. If all goes well, they move toward a commitment to the company's broader goals and ultimately to its "mission."

Rallying the troops is neither more nor less than an appeal to them to adopt the company's goals as their own.

"Instilling motivation" is a special case of instilling an attitude. The kind of motivation we mean is the kind that derives from full commitment. And the urge to commit oneself is best satisfied when it can be directed toward a clear and accessible object. Therefore instilling motivation is best done in the framework of a well-defined task—such as Pope's team had in producing the national parks book.

Justify Belief

There's a related goal that's less well known but equally vital to the smooth functioning of a goal-directed organization. Let's call it "justifying belief" or "justifying your partisans."

Suppose you find yourself standing in front of a group of people, all of whom already agree with you on the question at hand. Is there a persuasion opportunity here?

There could be, and it might be a pretty important one. These people, these "partisans" who agree with you, presumably mix with people who don't. Some of these latter people will be the dissenters or the disaffected inside your organization; others will be outsiders who see you unsympathetically. You can *equip your partisans to be effective advocates* by providing them with a full rationale of the goals and beliefs you hold in common.

Preachers of the Gospel do this all the time. They don't preach doctrines everybody has heard since childhood for their novelty; they preach them to justify and reinforce belief. This strengthens belief in the believer and gives him the raw material out of which to fashion his justification to nonbelievers.

To come down from the level of religion to the everyday world of business, let's imagine we're in Pope's editorial offices, and somebody from another book team asks a member of the national parks team what the project is all about. There's an unspoken question being asked: "Is your project worth the resources being devoted to it?"—resources that other teams might covet.

It's at this point that a team leader hopes he or she has fully justified the project to the team. If so, the member will be an effective advocate within the organization.

There's another goal closely related to this. It's the goal of making it intellectually respectable to be your partisan.

If you advocate a position that's held in contempt because it's new, untried, weird, eccentric, or countercultural, you may want to offer a full and detailed rationale to your partisans to help resolve their own doubts and to show the scoffers that there's more than one way to view the subject.

An appeal to authority can help in these cases. If "everybody" favors free trade and the "irrefutable" assumptions of the global economy ideal, it helps to be able to show that there are after all respectable economists and political leaders who doubt whether it's good for the workers in Gary, Indiana.

Soften Prejudice

Sometimes your persuasion goal will be to take apart what has been built up by decades of careless thinking: Ghetto kids won't work. Women make lousy cops. Middle-aged white males are antiwoman and antiblack.

The difficulty is that in the U.S. today nobody will admit that he harbors these stereotypes, except perhaps within the safety of a tight affinity group. In other words, nobody will expose such beliefs to criticism.

The best way to attack them is the Jackie Robinson way, by showing a counterexample that nobody can gloss over. The fact remains, though, that antiblack stereotypes persist these fifty years after Jackie Robinson made his first base hit for the Dodgers.

Prejudices die hard and softening them is no easy job. It may be best to deal with them indirectly, with a two-part attack. First, allude to Jackie Robinson–style examples that point out excellence where the stereotype says none should exist. And second, let it be known, if you're a team leader or thought-leader, that stereotypical thinking is dumb and has no place on your team.

What's "indirect" about this method is that it avoids the frontal assault. It calls for inductive rather than deductive thinking. It works because people who think in stereotypes—as we all do sometimes, on some subjects—deny to others and to themselves that they are doing so. If you offer the deductive argument based on the liberal theory of human equality, or on the U.S. Constitution, the stereotypers will of course agree and that'll be the end of it.

But examples, including the team leader's own example, force them to think and may change behavior. Even if all their private thinking amounts to is self-justification, they have vivid, disturbing examples before them and the leader has laid down a standard of right conduct that they must or should adhere to.

People do change, and often they change by being made to feel isolated and uncomfortable. They wake up to a choice between keeping the old idea or ending the discomfort.

Undermine the Opposition

When it appears that the opposition is making headway with a specious argument, you are fully justified in exposing its weakness or falsity.

In many cases you'll have no choice, since people under the influence of one opinion are often literally incapable of giving a fair hearing to another. Your only course is to undermine the preexisting position before setting forth your own.

It's best to start on the psychological level by acknowledging whatever genuine merit you can find in the opponent's case, and then by displaying a cheerful skepticism laced with a willingness to believe—if only you could. You then proceed to show why you can't, by moving to an exercise of pure reason if the case allows it. The best way to undermine the opponent is to demonstrate that he is contradicting himself. "He wants us to believe A. Yet he also proposes B. And we know that A and B are incompatible."

It is seldom as easy as that, but if you spot such an internal inconsistency, by all means call attention to it. More likely the inconsistency will be a matter of judgment, not simple logic. "He wants us to launch an expensive PR campaign to enhance our image in the community, but at the same time he is saying we should send three hundred jobs to China. Will it work? Is the public that stupid?"

Typically an internal contradiction reflects an unwillingness to live with the predictable consequences of one part of the argument. The second part is dragged in—as the PR campaign is dragged in in the example above—to show that the first part really has no adverse consequences or that they can be managed. Maybe they can. That's a question of judgment.

But in a case like this (assuming you're against the proposal) you have a right to probe the apparent contradiction, not on logical grounds but on the wisdom question.

"Maybe we *should* outsource the work. Let's leave that to one side for a minute. The question raised by this proposal is: if we do, can we really manage the backlash in the community by spending PR dollars?"

Your purpose is not to advance your own argument—not yet. It is to undermine his. This is one of the strictly limited persuasion goals that prepare the way for something more affirmative and ambitious, but at this moment your aim is to suggest that there may be something radically wrong with your opponent's case, since he seems to think he can avoid the unpleasant consequences of his basic recommendation.

Short of showing inconsistency, you can question the wisdom of an opponent's position by acknowledging that it does represent a perfectly reasonable program—"but is it the best we can do?"

You demonstrate that the payoff will not be so impressive as he claims, or merely that it *might* not be—implying that his faith is overextended. Then you are ready to advance a position that is equally reasonable, internally consistent, and promises a better payoff.

This isn't the place for an exhaustive treatment of ways to undermine an adversary. The essential point is that there are times when you *must do it* in order to gain a hearing for your own idea.

Test Your Thesis; Smoke Out Theirs

Sometimes the best use you can make of a persuasion opportunity is to test your thesis to strengthen it for future presentation to a more powerful audience.

Such testing is perhaps most successful when done before a splintered audience where the differences of opinion are purely professional and there's no personal animosity. An audience like that will offer mixed criticism and clear thinking. You could say: "Here's what I'd like to put on tomorrow's agenda, but I haven't yet been able to work out its full implications. I wonder what you think."

Your attitude should be objective and noncommittal. Quite probably you'll learn something about the strengths and weaknesses of your idea, as well as the tone and tenor of the reactions it elicits.

This kind of session also presents an opportunity to learn what others are thinking. Some of this will be implied in their critical comments and some will be stated explicitly and perhaps in a spirit of open competition. At all events the suppleness and versatility of your thesis will be tested and you will have moved a step forward.

If it's too weak for this audience, it certainly won't work higher up the line; if it is strengthened rather than weakened by criticism at this level, you can proceed with it more confidently.

And who knows? Today's critics may turn out to be tomorrow's partisans.

The second half of this goal—learning what the audience is thinking—is as important as the first. Sheila Sinclair makes an apt comment. She says she guards against a style of thinking that says, "I already know the answer." Even when she's virtually certain she knows what they think, *she asks the question anyway.*

The answers will often surprise you, and new and unanticipated material will flow into the dialogue in the wake of the answer. You ask about R. They give an answer on R that you never expected, and go on to tell you their thoughts and agendas on S and T.

The implication is clear. Don't be satisfied with what's in your own mind. Do your best to think clearly, creatively, and critically in the theater of your own mind, and then go out to the street and invite strangers in for the show. You will sometimes be amazed at the reaction.

Introduce Your Team

This is sometimes as important as presenting yourself, and it's a similar kind of job, with this notable difference: the people you introduce have to be a real team, not a collection of individuals. That makes it necessary for you and them to develop brief, vivid descriptions of their capabilities and experience so as to make it obvious why you chose them.

Unless your time is very limited *do not speak for them.* Let them speak for themselves. I've seen any number of team presentations marred by the dominating ego of the leader. Give them credit. Be proud of them. If you are integrating them into a presentation, make sure they have a truly substantive role to play.

And practice the handoffs. Be disciplined by the clock. Have a disinterested party critique each of you as individual performers and the team as a team.

Never degrade a team member by making her or him your chart-flipper—unless you take your own turn at the job. This shows mutual respect within the team and can be very impressive. You don't compromise your image as team leader by doing this, you strengthen it.

Communicate Your Passion

It's true: people like to do business with people who have a passion for their work. It follows that communicating that passion is a worthy persuasion goal. The problem then is how to do it.

We've already expressed the view that a direct report of your state of mind—"Wow, am I excited about our new product line!"—is not going to work, at least not by itself and certainly not as an opener. Try instead to take the listener through the same steps that led to your own passion.

This is easy enough to imagine if you're selling a 4 × 4 pick-up. What impresses you is its versatility. It'll plow through snow up to the axles or negotiate a granite staircase in Canyonlands National Park—yet take it out on the interstate and it rides like a Cadillac.

The best and perhaps only way to engender in your listener the same level of passion you feel is to take her through these steps. And a few restrained words of praise for the pickup will help her to interpret her experience the way you interpreted yours.

Or take Chris Stevens's business, brewed-by-the-cup coffee. Here again you have two benefits that at first might seem to exclude each other (quickness in the brewing and excellent taste); and the way to arouse the listener's interest, once again, perhaps the only way, is to brew her a cup and let her see a sparkling machine chugging away (for a mere thirty seconds), then taste the coffee.

At this point you (or Stevens) might say, "See why I'm in this business?"

I'd counsel a restrained expression of your enthusiasm because it's easier to err on the side of too much rather than too little. But this is a judgment only you the speaker can make. Try a careful modulation of your comments—let the *source* of your passion act directly on the listener when possible—and if you think you're coming on too subtle, turn up the heat.

You have to feel it yourself before you can expect others to feel it; and you have to find a way to put your dialogue partner in direct contact with the excellence that inspires you.

In the deal phase of Ricci's Triad this can be done with numbers; in the concept phase with elegance of presentation; and in the people phase by Subject Mastery and the other elements of the persuasive persona.

There's another way to communicate passion: the story.

You were bedeviled by a software problem. The whole office was groaning. You and a friend began tinkering with a solution. You borrowed money. Your husband and your partner's wife pitched in. You borrowed more money. You built a prototype, hired an engineer, improved the prototype. Your partner's wife had a baby—the baby and your first Beta site came at the same time. You quit your day job. You had $3,000 left when you filled the first order.

"And now, would you like to see what this new software will do?"

Of course he already has a general idea what it'll do but now when he sees it in action he'll have a keener appreciation of it because of the empathy you instilled by telling a story with real characters, suspense, and a climax.

Control the Atmosphere

There will be times when the atmosphere in a room is not conducive to your goals. There'll be too much levity, too much confusion, noise, seriousness, stress, anxiety, formality, anger, impatience—too much or too little of something.

You can influence and in some cases control the atmosphere by your own demeanor, by calling attention to the agenda, by referring to the accomplishments of competitors—by somehow focusing minds on an idea with implications that tend to have the psychological effects you desire.

If a meeting is falling apart because of intellectual confusion, you can intervene to bring about clarity. For example, "It seems to me that we're making an unconscious assumption. We're all assuming that our suppliers are incapable of meeting this accelerated schedule. If they are, we really do face the problem we all seem to be concerned about. But do we really know this? Let's call a couple of suppliers and find out."

The meeting is now focused on a question of fact: can the suppliers meet the schedule? Instead of generalized consternation there's likely to be an atmosphere of "let's find out."

It's not possible to write an all-purpose formula for achieving a change of atmosphere, but you ought sometimes to try changing it *before* you try to achieve some other goal. And remember: if people are tired and hungry, coffee and danish can work wonders.

Display an Opportunity
Before people can act they need a reason to believe an opportunity exists, and opportunities are sometimes disguised. Famously, they come in the disguise of a problem, but the more common cover is the action vacuum.

"Nothing going on here, no activity or energy, so let's go somewhere else." But wait a minute. *Why* isn't there anything going on?

Chris Stevens's coffee-in-the-office opportunity is a good example. For decades, in fact centuries, people have been glumly drinking lousy coffee in the office; there didn't seem to be any other choice. But recently the quality brands have shown that coffee addicts need not suffer during working hours. All they have to do (if they've got the time) is to sneak out for a cup of the real thing. Still there has been little or no "action" in the office itself. It was a place to work or horse around, but not drink really satisfying coffee.

What Stevens and his competitors did was to redefine this dead zone as an opportunity.

A speaker who wants to initiate action in a dead zone can do no better than to start by surveying the situation, taking note of the curious lack of activity, then redefining the action vacuum as an invitation to act.

Position Yourself for Future Influence
When vocabulary and agenda are clearly under somebody else's control, whether that somebody is friendly or hostile, your first

thought may be that there's no gain to be had in this drama. But let's look closer. Even if it's true that you're out of the action today, is there a chance here to build a position for tomorrow?

By helping to clarify the group's goals, for example, you might do a present service and display Subject Mastery. Somebody is going to notice. You will thus make yourself a person worth listening to, even if your own agenda (spoken or not) is ignored.

You can also position yourself for future influence merely by using a natural opportunity, should one arise, to display competence. You might address a Mexican salesman in his native language. The monolingual people will make a mental note: "This person speaks Spanish. Maybe she can help out at next week's meeting."

Or you can volunteer to take on part of the work. This is a good way to enter the action, and it's done with a special good grace when it's known that you had other goals in mind but are playing team ball by volunteering.

At the most basic level you position yourself for future influence by showing 1) team spirit and 2) valuable personal attributes.

One of our underlying themes in this chapter has been that there's a kind of craftsmanship in setting goals. It's true, as we said earlier, that they pop into your head as a rhyme pops into the poet's head or a tune greets a happily surprised composer. How this sort of thing happens is mysterious. It feels like luck. We say of the poet or tunesmith that he or she has a knack for it. We seldom try to explain it.

But to some degree we all make our own luck. We have already seen that there are ways to test goals, to weed out the useless or diversionary, and to keep your activity *directed* by goals that offer a chance of leading toward the power-benefit handshake.

Without venturing into the foggy lowlands of psychology, we must now ask if there is a way to *stimulate* our minds to produce goals. Presumably the goals or goal-candidates so produced will still need to be examined by SMAC + Essentiality + Bounce (+ Instinct!)—they won't all be golden; there'll be a lot of brass and a little lead mixed in.

But you'll still feel better about goal D if you have a chance to compare it to E, F, and G before you adopt it. So there's a net plus in generating multiple goals and then deciding which are most promising.

I'd liken it to a CEO who has asked his creative people to design a new company logo. While he doesn't claim any special artistic talent, he's a guy who knows what he likes, and he intends to make the final choice himself. The creative people would be nuts to present him only one candidate. Even if he liked it he would almost certainly demand a few other choices. And if he didn't like it he'd say, "Is this all you've got, *one idea?*"

We all like to believe that we pursue a goal not merely because it popped into our head but because we judge it worthy of our efforts.

Let's see how Jim Groom, the "best-idea-wins" architect, stimulates his own and his clients' minds to generate goals.

Like any conscientious professional he operates under the general guidance of a mission statement or professional vision. From an addition to the main library at a university to a remodeling job on a ski chalet, Groom puts his name on his work forever. Therefore the *pride* that is the reward of excellence is a goal concurrent with all others. We summarize his (unwritten) mission statement like this: excellence in design, execution, and service to the client.

How does this play out in a typical project?

Perhaps the most striking thing about Groom's methodology is how similar it is to Eric Giler's. Giler, the founder of a high-tech manufacturing firm, goes as deep as he can into the mind of the dialogue partner as a way of moving to the power-benefit handshake. Jim Groom, working in what might seem like a very different business, starts by trying to get clients to "communicate their dream."

He asks them to fill out a ten-page questionnaire; he has long talks with them; he notes any differences that emerge, in the case of a couple, between one party and the other; he walks around the site with them, and if it's a remodeling job, he tries to see what they appreciate most about the old place and what they most want to change.

When he finally switches on his computer, he already knows a lot about their wants and needs. Then he produces a set of sketches.

These might present five, six, or seven possibilities, maybe more. At the next meeting he goes over the sketches with the clients—and here he likens his role to a standup comedian who is constantly trying to read the audience. What do they like? What do they appreciate? "I'm watching their faces," Groom says.

Client and architect discuss the options, but "words are never enough. Eventually somebody has to draw something."

So he begins revising the sketches freehand, or drawing new ones. His drawings depict changes and innovations large and small, and the clients react.

"I might rip it up and say, 'Let's try it another way,' watching all the time."

The process goes on, with the clients moving toward a clearer vision of what they want and Groom toward a firmer grasp of the aesthetics and economics of the project. It's out of this process that architect and clients agree on the scope, design, and timetable of the project. Hundreds of subordinate decisions are wrapped into the plan agreed upon in meetings like these.

And if all goes well, the parties will have found a broad compatibility of goals at the action level, stimulated by Groom's pursuit of lesser goals at the persuasion level.

What's going on here, clearly, is careful, persistent audience analysis *plus* a judicious use of persuasion techniques to move the parties toward a mutually acceptable (beneficial) definition of the project.

The method appears to subordinate Groom's interests to the clients', but in fact they stand as equals at the moment of the handshake. At that moment both architect and client agree to pursue mutually beneficial goals. Had Groom started by trying to impose his vision on the client the outcome might not have been so happy.

We've now come to the curious part, and in some ways the really revealing moment, in our examination of goals.

All these things the persuader has been doing for himself he is really doing for others as well. If he really has something of value to offer—a benefit—then by moving the audience toward agreement he moves them toward something they themselves will define as good when they get there.

It starts with the clients looking around and seeing that Groom does, in their own terms, "good work." Something good lies at the end of the dialogue. They open talks with him because they sense this possibility. All parties move toward the handshake and all feel they have done the right thing.

This suggests that the persuader's goals are linked somehow to the benefits he or she offers. The goals, when achieved, carry the parties toward the handshake. It follows that a persuader can generate goals for herself—guide her persuasion effort—by pondering the benefit she offers and then looking for ways to make it visible to the audience.

It's not so simple as a pure and unprepared display of the benefit. Rather it's a job of preparing the audience to appreciate the benefit when seen.

Groom's clients, like Giler's investors—or like the person you want to bring on board as a partner or employee—have to be *ready to appreciate* the benefit, and this readiness is a state of mind that is created gradually and *voluntarily*. A mind cannot be forced.

But if you really have a benefit to offer—if you believe in your own ability, your team, your product—then it ought to be possible to fashion and pursue persuasion goals that will open the eyes of your dialogue partner to the genuine merits of your offering.

The close attention that Groom, Giler, Sinclair, and other good persuaders pay to their audiences suggests that the more intimately you understand your audience and the more you encourage dialogue with them, the better your chance of reaching the power-benefit handshake.

The need to know and respect your listener, and to invite interaction between your mind and his, is never more critical than in the argument phase of a persuasion drama. Now we get to the heart of the matter. Now we're ready to see how an argument ticks—how the intellect appeals to the emotions, how the emotions stimulate the intellect, and how facts with legs turn information into energy.

4

Making Your Case —
The Argument as a Means
of Persuasion

Presenting an argument is a little like painting an old boat. You have to prepare the surface before you start painting. If the sailor's first step is to open the can and dip in his brush, he might as well throw the paint overboard. He may be ready but the boat is not. First it needs to be scraped, sanded, and primed. Until it is, it simply won't take the paint.

Our minds are the same way. They won't "take" an argument until they're ready. The speaker may have gathered and arranged his evidence and worked out his logic to perfection; he may have drafted an argument that's a marvel of eloquence, conciseness, and power. But if the listener doesn't really listen, nothing is going to happen in the only place where it counts—the mind of the listener.

So what can a speaker do? Just as a sailor has to prepare the surface before he starts painting, a persuader has to prepare the surface of a listener's mind before he can hope to penetrate the interior.

THE "INTRODUCTION"

That's why the Greeks and Romans taught their citizen-orators to open a presentation with something that we today would call an introduction.

The persuasion goal of the introduction is not to get rolling on a narration of the facts; it is not to state a thesis; and it is not to give some kind of preview of the argument—although a speaker may well decide that a thesis or preview serves his purpose quite well. But what is his purpose?

It is to *gain a fair hearing* for his argument.

In other words a speaker who is about to present an argument—a buildup of reasoning—that she has constructed precisely *to appeal to the listener's rationality,* a speaker who has built her case out of hard facts and tight logic, this same woman sets herself an initial persuasion goal that is partly an *appeal to emotion.*

She does not abandon her commitment to reason; she merely recognizes that there may be obstacles standing between her and the reasoning part of her listener's mind. If she's a knowing and rational speaker, she will do what she can to level those obstacles. *Then* she can move to her argument, which is a *process of reasoning* from a factual basis.

So how does she go about leveling the obstacles—how does she achieve the persuasion goal of gaining an unprejudiced hearing for her argument? Nobody will be surprised to hear that her first step is to gain the respect and trust of the audience.

Some readers may be thinking, "That's easy for you to say," and certainly it's easier said than done. But there *are* ways to do it, many previously covered in the section devoted to the persuasive persona. What we're examining now is a special case of self-presentation, and self-presentation is a natural combination of god-given personality and art.

We've seen that your real, genuine personality is a great asset— so long as it is genuine. The role of art is not to distort but to strengthen that personality as it enters the persuasion drama. One way to strengthen it is to take what we have learned about the persuasive persona and apply it to this special goal of winning a fair hearing.

Our immediate task, then, is simply to observe the elements of the persuasive persona (Subject Mastery, Steadiness, Ability, Empathy, Candor) going to work in a few examples. Chapter 1 argued that the character of the speaker is a prime persuader. Character plays a key role in pre-persuasion too.

Three examples will be enough to show how it works. The principle is the same whether in a standup presentation, colloquy, or dialogue.

Imagine the effect when General Schwartzkopf walks into the officers' club. The moment he's seen, he owns the place, whether he came to persuade anybody of anything or just to have dinner.

He has gained respect and trust by virtue of a *reputation* that conveys all the elements of the persuasive persona. For people who worry about their proficiency as speakers there's a cheering lesson in this.

You build reputation by performance over a whole career—not by being quick, glib, and witty but by being reliable and right. It follows that anybody can reach the persuasion goal of gaining a fair hearing. It may take some luck, but perseverance and honest work will stretch luck into the kind of reputation that opens others' minds to your argument.

Your whole career and history are in this sense a preparation for whatever persuasion challenge you face on a given day. Your career is a lifelong opportunity to project Subject Mastery, Ability, and the other elements of the persuasive persona. Your reputation is the distillate of your achievement. The "introduction" is already behind you; you can count on a fair hearing for your ideas.

Usually, but not always, the kind of reputation that opens minds is a reputation for Subject Mastery existing in a benign combination with Empathy. Schwartzkopf is admired not only because he won the Gulf War but because of his well-known concern for the safety and welfare of his troops. His reputation is a channel for communicating Subject Mastery and Empathy.

Our second example is Chris Stevens's performance before that big crowd of influential businesspeople.

He was working on two interlocking goals: to give a solid critique of the brewer's business operation and to show his own company's flag. For the first maybe, for the second definitely, *he had to open minds*.

The evening's printed program carried three or four lines about Chris and the other speakers but nowhere near enough to establish the kind of reputation that is its own introduction. So he had to adopt some other strategy. He chose to dazzle the audience and, because he has that talent, it worked.

Let's put it this way. By giving a dazzling, witty, and entertaining performance he gained their sympathy and approval, thus achieving the goal of gaining a fair hearing for his critique. And the critique itself was a sound piece of work.

And because Stevens is V.P. of marketing and sales for his startup, *the performance was direct evidence of his competence* in his profession. His success in opening their minds was already the beginning of success in putting across his implicit thesis, that his firm was run by a team of first-rate people.

Dazzling talent is pretty rare but there's another way to gain an unprejudiced hearing that is open to practically everybody.

For our third example we return to Barbara Piette, the venture capitalist we quoted earlier on the subject of empathy. Like Steve Ricci she has literally hundreds of entrepreneurs clamoring for her attention. If she said to each one, "All right, I will judge you on your argument—that after all is the heart of your case—so let's see your evidence and logic," she'd never make a dime for her investors. She'd be a perpetual audience.

Obviously her first job is to decide who to listen to. Here's one of the ways she does it. She glances at the business plan. If it looks promising, she picks up the phone and calls the entrepreneur. He may be caught off guard or he may be prepared for just such a call (he should be). Says Piette, "Those first ten minutes are incredibly important."

She may want the entrepreneur to elaborate on the written plan but she is after bigger game than that. She has placed the call with a specific and critical question in mind: is this person capable of articulating the plan?

If the answer is no, end of story. If it's yes, she schedules a meeting to give the entrepreneur a chance to expound the plan at length. These meetings typically last an hour and a half, showing that Piette is really serious—really listening.

So Piette has made the decision to listen—to open her mind—based partly on an impromptu "introduction" from the entrepreneur. And the entrepreneur/speaker has achieved the threshold goal of gaining a fair hearing by demonstrating a certain style of Subject Mastery.

Those "incredibly important" minutes on the phone are sometimes boiled down to *a few seconds.* Jim Geisman, a business consultant to high-tech ventures, is a great proponent of a simple but surprisingly severe test, the "elevator pitch."

He asks you to imagine you're in an elevator and the man beside you says, "Tell me about your business." Obviously he's not soliciting a whole business plan since the building only has ten floors and you're passing the fifth. How do you respond? It will depend on who the man is—an investor, prospective employee, salesperson, etc. But here are some all-purpose possibilities.

"I run a medical transcription service. We transcribe chart and office notes, histories, and physicals and get them back to the doctor in twenty-four hours, faster if necessary."

"I run a junk-computer placement service. You give me your old machine. I put it in good working order, using cannibalized parts if necessary, then I find a certified charity and donate it. I give them a thirty-day guarantee and you an affidavit showing who got it and how much it was worth."

"My partner and I have developed a cleaner, safer way to remove lead paint from old houses that new owners are remodeling. We are seeking financing and regulatory approval, and we are already talking with some of the big painting contractors about a risk-free tryout."

Each of these can be spoken in less than fifteen seconds and each couples a benefit with a beneficiary. Each states a clear business concept without loading on the details.

We read the one about the medical transcription business to Geisman and he made a suggestion. He said a good pitch will differentiate the business from competitors. He suggested it would be stronger if it offered transcription service, for example, to medical research labs, where the vocabulary and subject matter might be pretty rarefied.

The implication is that if you examine your pitch and find it too generic, maybe the same criticism applies to your business concept. If you find your pitch is too detailed, maybe you haven't clarified your core function in your own mind.

The elevator pitch is useful to both speaker and listener. For the speaker it offers a form of discipline that drives him back to the center and origin of all his thoughts about his business. It forces him to articulate his central concepts. For the listener it offers a clear, simple statement of the business purpose being served, and an opportunity to evaluate the speaker.

Geisman says, "If he cannot state in succinct terms via simple declarative statements what he's trying to do and why he's doing it, chances are he's not doing it very well."

An elevator pitch raises more questions than it answers but they are likely to be questions about how the business works, not what it is. Thus the questions lead to focused dialogue.

Take Geisman's own elevator pitch. "Marketshare, Inc. is a business development consultancy." He usually pauses here, to see the effect of that tantalizing phrase "business development consultancy." The next part is: "We work with software companies to help them do more business faster in the U.S. and Japan."

Depending on the audience, and particularly on the stage of development of the businesses they represent, these two sentences generate a variety of questions and call for additional messages.

"The purpose of the elevator pitch," in Geisman's view, "is to attempt to plant the seed and fertilize the ground at the same time."

Or put it this way. The purpose is to state your concept clearly but *provocatively*—to provoke questions and generate dialogue centered on your core concept and activities. Dialogue like:

"Hmmm—the doctor gets clean copy the next day?"

"Yes."

"And your people can handle specialized vocabulary?"

"Yes."

"Well, did you ever think of—. Listen, why couldn't you do the same for lawyers?"

"We probably could. Why don't you tell me what you need."

That's productive dialogue. That's how a finely tuned elevator pitch can gain you a hearing from a real listener.

PLANTING DOUBT

There are listeners—actually nonlisteners—who are perfectly content with their existing stock of ideas. More than content, they're desperately happy with what's already inside their heads and they regard new ideas as a social disease.

Of course there's a little of this tendency in all of us. We adhere to Proposition X for what seem like good and sufficient reasons. If somebody proposes Anti-X we react against him more or less automatically, and it's natural we should. How could we maintain continuity of action and character if we changed our minds every minute? It's built into our mental lives that we should advance in stages toward belief in X (or move away) and, having attained a feeling of certainty, stick with it.

So how is any such person—whether pigheaded or just firmly committed—ever to be persuaded that Better-than-X or Different-from-X exists and deserves his or her consideration? How, to be more specific, do you as an operator in the business world crack a mind made of stone?

The process by which such minds are changed is elegantly presented in a famous essay titled "The Fixation of Belief," published in *Popular Science Monthly* in 1877. The author was the American mathematician and philosopher Charles Sanders Peirce.

Peirce argues that a closed mind is a happy mind. And the way to open it is to make it a little less happy.

This is easily done if we are able to implant doubt about the beliefs and conclusions that are the source of the mind's complacency. Peirce says that all humans can feel the difference between *doubt* and *belief*. Having reached a belief, we want to keep it because belief feels good; doubt is unpleasant and makes us restless and discontent. Whenever we find ourselves in doubt we *struggle* (Peirce's word) to reach a new shore of belief. Doubt is a turbulent ocean; belief is a serene and green landscape.

So how do you plant doubt? We are, after all, talking about some guy who's quite pleased with what's already in his head.

Peirce goes about it this way. He says that we all recognize that reasoning is solid when it leads to true conclusions. We reject reasoning that leads to conclusions that can be shown to be false. And in Peirce's world there is one and only one way to test truth and falsehood, and that way is the scientific method. He appeals to us not to be intoxicated with guiding principles or methodology, or overawed by authority or the mob, but to test our conclusions against rigorous standards of scientific verification. *Plant doubt* means don't bother (not yet) with the other guy's reasoning, his authorities, his alliances, or his facts. Don't argue about whether his facts justify his belief. Go right to his conclusion/belief and drive a wedge in by attacking the "scientific" verifiability of the belief itself.

At this stage of any argument it's too early to try to demolish his belief, let alone advance your own. Be content at this stage to plant doubt, *because doubt agitates the mind.*

Peirce's method is even more powerful today than in his own era. In the century and a quarter since he wrote "The Fixation of Belief" an elementary scientific method has become the common property of every educated person. A conclusion that's not verifiable, particularly one that can't be replicated in unbiased inquiry, is automatically suspect.

It's no longer good enough to defend your belief as "agreeable to reason" or "in harmony with natural law" or "proven by long practice." If a belief is all or any of these it should be able to endure the toughest scrutiny. A belief that cannot is downgraded to the status of a mere personal preference.

And yet business is not science, so what we have to ask if we want to use this potent weapon that Peirce makes available is whether in the world of business (preeminently a world of judgments) there is any method or test that can stand in the place Peirce assigns to scientific method. There may be business "incubators" and business "laboratories" but the businessperson operates in a world where it's impossible to say, "Hold on there, Knute, while I hire a bunch of scientists to test your stubbornly held opinion."

If there were a standard short of scientific verifiability and yet *capable of reducing fixed belief to the status of mere preference* it would make the tactic of planting doubt an excellent way to gain a hearing, both from the person holding the fixed belief and from the spectators, if you're going on display.

If there were such a standard, it would be flexible enough to apply truly scientific reasoning where appropriate (actuarial science is one instance) but it would also be capable of giving due weight to the human element.

Is there such a standard?

Let's look for our answer in the work experience of Susan C. Hammond, chief financial officer for several small companies. As we examine Hammond's experience we should keep in mind that we aren't looking for a formula or algorithm, such as might work in a laboratory, but for a real-world kind of touchstone that will work in the realm of wisdom that we call the business world.

When she made the jump from big-firm accounting to CFO work for small clients, Hammond got into a different ball game. Her clients typically generate less than $1 million in sales a year, and their size dictates two operating characteristics: 1) strategic decisions are made by individuals, often by one person, without the aid or interference of bureaucracies; and 2) every dollar counts.

Taken together these realities create an important strategic role for the CFO. Hammond finds herself searching out the strategic implications of financial decisions and the financial implications of strategic decisions. This same reciprocity applies in big companies too but is intensified and highlighted in smaller outfits where a decision like the lease on a copying system is a major expense.

Hammond's business card tells the story. It doesn't say "part-time CFO." It says "CFO Strategies . . . Strategic Solutions for Business Growth." She views business problems *through the lens of finance.* This gives her a way to test the rationality or even the wisdom of those decisions.

She asks whether the proposed action makes good business sense —and as a CFO she has a reasonably concrete (almost scientific) way to answer the question. She says, "I spend a lot of my time asking clients, 'Does what you're doing make sense?'" and then she tests how sensible it is in terms of the company's financial position.

At first hearing that sounds too simple or maybe too vague to be useful, but what she's trying to do is to fit a proposal into a program of future business action. She encourages the client to look beyond the horizon and to remember that business programs are fueled and constrained by money. Here's one example.

A client had decided to hire a consultant Hammond thought was unsuitable. She opposed the decision, and the client simply reiterated her determination. The client's message was: this work has got to be done and this person can do it so I'm hiring him.

In our terms, Hammond's problem was to gain a hearing. Not to argue for some other action, not yet, but simply to gain access to the decision-maker's mind.

She could have attacked the decision on the facts. She could have asserted that the work did *not* have to be done, that this person couldn't do it, or that the client hadn't interviewed enough candidates. Any of these might have worked, but all the signs pointed to a mind unreceptive to new facts or reexamination of the "established" ones.

So Hammond tried what we call planting doubt for the limited purpose of opening the decision-maker's mind. What she did was, in our view, pretty remarkable. She asked the client: if you had all the staff you needed, would this person fit in?

We can imagine a pause while the client grasps the implications of the question: whether we do or don't need somebody, is this person a good choice *for our team* in the long run?

And Hammond followed up with: because if you hire him and he doesn't fit into the company culture, or if he's not as good as you think, "he'll be learning on our nickel."

We'll learn the outcome of this drama in the next chapter, when we take up the subject of meeting resistance. For now our point is that Hammond planted "the irritation of doubt" — by suggesting the decision might waste the company's money.

Her question was provocative: if you didn't need this guy, would you still want him around? In that question the money factor and the human factor ride side by side. If he can't fit in with existing staff, he's a bad choice whether you need him or not; and if he's a bad choice — in Hammond's words — "the money has gone out the door" and the company has not received service of value in return.

Hammond was thinking as entrepreneurs must think, across all functions, and speaking with the authority of a CFO trained in quantitative reasoning.

If planting doubt fails, the decision-maker's mind is right where it was before, and the persuader hasn't lost any ground. If it succeeds, the decision-maker starts wrestling with doubt and trying to reach the safety of belief. In other words, the persuader has made an opening for her argument.

There are other ways to plant doubt about an entrenched belief.

You can cheerfully admit the facts and show that some other conclusion might also follow from them. You can point out that a respected authority looked at the case or a similar one and drew a different conclusion, or that the conclusion/opinion is inconsistent with some other opinion held by the same believer. You may say that the believer himself held a different opinion only last week, that the conclusion was reached in haste, or that it was reached so slowly as to imply that some objections were especially hard to overcome. You could suggest that it coincides all too neatly with somebody's interests or that people who study it end up less enthusiastic than they began.

The doubt need not be strong enough to topple the believer's whole edifice or to expose its cracks and flaws immediately. All it has to do is make the believer or spectators uneasy. This will let you pull them into what Peirce called Inquiry and give you a better chance of presenting your argument to real listeners.

The stratagem of planting doubt is not a silver bullet. Some people are incapable of listening and some commitments are everlasting. But in a high percentage of cases in which the listener starts the drama by showing a closed mind, a deftly placed doubt will tend to dissolve his certainty.

We have examined this in detail because the commonest of all persuasion mistakes is to jump to the argument before the listener is ready. Speakers often do even worse: they blurt out their main *conclusion* first. The other guy immediately rejects it, maybe even ridicules it, and the chance for a fluid, *moving* dialogue is all but lost. One party has stated, "X," and the other has said, "Oh no, not X. Not on your life!"

The tactic of planting doubt, employed in appropriate cases, recognizes the twin truths of Peirce's doctrine—that belief is comfortable (we cling to it) and that doubt is irritating (we commence an inquiry to bring it to an end).

Before leaving Peirce let's glance at something we've touched on once or twice before. Even if the doubt fails to stir uneasiness and to initiate inquiry in the believer it may well do so *in the spectators.* Therefore planting doubt in a meeting, colloquy, or dialogue before an audience can be very effective. You plant doubt and present your argument—ostensibly to the stubborn believer, but actually you're *on display*, and your real audience is the third parties whose doubt about the preexisting belief is much stronger than the believer's. Their minds are receptive.

You can undermine the believer's position, reduce his credibility while building yours, and in the end shake the believer's confidence when he sees the others beginning to array themselves against him. You can also win allies, and they may help out by adding evidence and reasoning to strengthen your argument.

TWO LITTLE WORDS

And those two words—*evidence* and *reasoning*—are all the definition we need of an argument. We're not taking about a dispute, a controversy, or a fistfight, but about a process of reasoning wherein the speaker offers evidence and shows what it means.

Dictators, frauds, bullies, and gangsters exact consent by means of fear, trickery, or violence. They do not present arguments and they don't really persuade. They control behavior by terrorizing or paralyzing the minds of human beings, but they do not lead minds into new paths.

Some textbooks of logic, for the sake of completeness, will mention arguments by coercion, threat, or force, but exacting consent and winning a mind's allegiance are not the same. An argument that is truly a process of reasoning from agreed evidence can lead a mind to some *new vantage point* from which a *new path* is visible. And if the argument also exhibits the *appeal* of the new path, then it has brought the listener to the *threshold of action.*

And *action* of course is the aim of persuasion in business—as it is in the military, a university faculty committee, or any organization that has been created to get something done.

So we can say that an *effective argument* is one that leads the listener to the new vantage point and shows the way to some desirable action. And since we are animals who are identified partly by our delight in learning, an argument can even instill the incentive to follow the new path.

This is due to a strange and happy coincidence. We do not resent or fight those who persuade us. In the very act of persuading they have convinced us. And this convincing is an identity-reinforcing experience for us, the listeners. We feel ourselves taking over the process as we digest the facts and assent to the reasoning. We see the merit of the argument, and seeing it we associate ourselves with it. We like what we're doing.

A man somehow convinces me he would be a damned good advocate for me in a legal fight, and I'm glad to learn it. A salesperson gives an energy-packed demonstration of the superiority of some new computer over my present machine, and I get excited. I admire her as a presenter, which brings me close to admiring her as a person.

In assenting to an argument, in saluting its evidence and embracing its reasoning, we do not feel diminished, we feel confirmed. Even when we give our consent reluctantly (because we're not prepared to face the consequences) we are still conscious of having done the right thing in consenting. We have not been beaten by the persuader, we have joined her freely. We are moving toward action.

If action is to be motivated and sustained, it must be voluntary. And this voluntariness—this respect for the autonomy of the listener—is the whole reason that a hierarchical superior will argue a case to his or her subordinates instead of barking orders. John Pope of Reader's Digest does not bark orders. Some people think that dictating action is more efficient than inspiring it, and they are wrong.

Even military officers and NCOs, the good ones, seldom bark orders outside of boot camp. Subordinates will usually obey but nobody likes the feeling of obeying. A superior who wants his people to devote themselves to the goals he articulates will show them the grounds for devotion.

Susan Hammond says, "I hate to be told anything. You have to show me."

This showing is the role of the argument.

COMPLETING THE CIRCUIT

An argument is intertwined with emotions, especially feelings of hope and need, and it gains force from the character of the speaker, but its inner circuitry is intellectual. No matter how long or elaborate an argument may be, the current always flows in a predetermined pattern, and the pattern is simple.

It has to be. When our minds seek an explanation or a reason we should agree with somebody, we don't want to be confronted with a mass of squiggles, fishhooks, and boxes from symbolic logic. What we want is simplicity and soundness, and that's what we get in a skillfully presented argument.

Such an argument works like an electric circuit. Here stands an electrode, all by itself. It seems to be dead. We move it toward another similarly "dead" electrode and as they approach each other we sense that something is about to happen. Suddenly the two are joined by a crackling flash. The current has leapt the gap and completed the circuit, releasing energy in the form of light.

Our minds work the same way. One fact alone is inert, mere information. Couple it with another in just the right way and *zap!* — the current leaps the gap, closes the circuit, and releases a flash of light in which we can see something that wasn't there before, something called a *conclusion.* Those dull, inert facts were charged all along but the energy was trapped until they came together.

We'll see this happening in the following true persuasion drama. The names and some details have been changed to protect the guilty.

It was a dark and stormy night on the river but the water was gentle and calm. The tempest was all inside the cruise boat. From the shore it must have looked like a floating Chinese lantern and sounded like a riot set to music.

It was in fact a celebration by forty people who had been looking at unemployment a week ago and were now secure in jobs that had turned to gold when the startup got its first big order. The musicians alternated the body-rubbing numbers with chances for serious solo and pair dancing, which sometimes approached frenzy.

But even the best of office parties has to end, and as the boat approaches the dock we'll pause to name the main characters in our drama. They are:

> SANDRA, a trial lawyer; wife of the CEO; not otherwise connected with the company.
> PETER, an intellectual-property lawyer; outside counsel to the company.
> DAVE, an electrical engineer and member of the CEO's original team; stakeholder in the company.
> (The CEO, BRUCE, drank himself out of a role.)

SCENE 1

The musicians stopped playing so as not to disturb the people sleeping in the apartment houses along the channel. The skipper throttled back. The line handler jumped ashore to make his ties. The party was over.

Dave took a while leaving. He had been struck with a sudden hunger and began scavenging the ruins of the buffet. Finding nothing good he finally turned to the gangway, said his good-byes, and stepped to the dock. But an urgent call from Sandra halted him. He turned around.

She was standing at the other end of the gangway supporting her CEO husband.

"Stop him!" she cried.

"Stop who?"

"Peter. There he goes. Quick."

Dave saw Peter walking away like a man with confusion and pain in his head and eggs in his shoes. He called, "Hey, Peter!" and Peter kept on going.

"Stop him! We can't let him drive home."

"Oh—he's O.K.," said Dave without really caring whether he was O.K. or not.

"He is not O.K. He can't drive like that."

Dave chased Peter down and talked to him. Could he drive? Was he in control? Could he count backwards? Yes, yes, yes.

Returning to the pier Dave told Sandra: "He's O.K. He says he's a careful driver. He says he does it all the time."

"If he kills somebody their heirs will sue us!"

"Well—maybe—sure, but . . ."

Now she fairly screamed, "We'll lose everything!"

Dave didn't answer and Sandra said it again with more gusto.

"Sure," Dave insisted, "but he doesn't seem all that drunk."

"He was tripping all over the place. Didn't you see him?"

"No," Dave admitted as his mind began to turn on its axis.

"Sure. He fell against a table and knocked off all the glasses."

"He did?"

"He fell on Bruce." (her wavering husband)

"He did?"

"Stop him for God's sake."

Dave turned to go after Peter, but Peter was gone.

How the Circuit Is Completed in Scene 1

Something happened in Dave's mind to move him from indifference to the conviction that he had to act. What was it? Sandra persuaded him, but how?

First, whether deliberately or not, she displayed her own sense of urgency. She didn't succeed in communicating it to Dave, who wasn't ready to receive it, but at least he saw that she felt it.

She told him her first "fact"—that Peter couldn't drive. Dave then questioned Peter and returned unimpressed. In other words he rejected this fact. A fact to her, fiction to him.

Seeing that Dave was unmoved Sandra raised the voltage by trying to involve him emotionally—"Someone could sue us! . . . We'll lose everything!" But Dave still didn't get it.

In her own mind Sandra had completed a circuit that looked like this:

1. Partygivers are responsible for their drunks.

2. Peter is our drunk.

3. *Therefore* we are responsible for Peter.

Believing (accepting) 1 and 2, she was *compelled* to accept them together—as a dynamic pair. This compulsion carried her forward to 3, the conclusion that the company was responsible for Peter.

Her problem was to make Dave see the case as she saw it. What did she do?

As a lawyer Sandra had no doubts about number 1. She knew it had made its way into the law and that cases upholding the principle that partygivers are responsible for their drunks had received wide publicity. She made a tactical assumption that Dave probably accepted 1; so she concentrated on making him believe 2, that Peter really was drunk. If she could convince him of that, then the two facts, 1 and 2, would come together in his mind, the arc would close, and he would see the same conclusion she saw, as well as give it the emotional value she did.

So she raised the voltage again by piling on evidence that Peter was indeed drunk. It was this new evidence thrown into the scales to support 2 that changed Dave's mind. He turned to catch Peter but Peter was gone.

Maybe Dave could have reasoned out the conclusion as soon as Sandra did, but he didn't care. The new evidence brought the conclusion smack into his own life. It made him see the whole sequence 1, 2, 3 more vividly *because it aroused an emotion* in him: fear. A purely intellectual construct, a mere switching device, was now blazing with emotion.

SCENE 2

Dave set out along a walkway leading from the dock toward the street. The walk had stores and offices on either side, but at this hour the only light came from the dock behind him and from the street ahead. He could not see anyone in the half-dark stretch between him and the street.

Just before he reached the end of the walk he saw what he took to be a homeless man slumped in an angle of the building to his left—and with a little *flip* in his gut he approached. Neither spoke until Dave stood within three paces.

"Peter, what are you doing?"

Peter declared he wasn't doing anything.

"You're under arrest. I'm driving you home."

"No, ridiculous. I've never had an accident in my life."

"Come on. My car's around the corner."

"Never. I'd have to take a cab down here tomorrow to get my car and I'll be damned—"

"Listen, Peter my man, we're responsible for you, you know that."

"Blah blah blah."

"I can't let you drive home."

"Blah blah . . ."

"Look at you. You're blotto."

"Blah—uh—blah . . ."

"Sandra wants me to drive you home."

A stare, but not a blank stare, from Peter: Sandra, hmm. Sandra, a lawyer herself, wife of the CEO . . .

"She says we could all be ruined," said Dave.

"Baloney," Peter replied but something had happened to his bravado.

"Baloney my foot. You're a lawyer; think about it."

"With this head?"

"There's my point. Listen, Peter, Sandra is afraid we could lose everything. She's really pissed."

"Aaaaah, grmf, grmf—where is it?"

"Where is what?"

"Your car, propellerhead."

"Right this way, counselor."

Completing the Circuit in Scene 2

Here, as in the first scene, there is more than one fact pair driving events, but only one that takes the drunken Peter to a new vantage point from which he sees the reason for giving in. He might have been longing for bed, or for another drink, or breakfast. There's a lot happening mentally, and when you unmask the forces driving the drama you are struck with wonder that the mind can work so fast. But *something* chased everything else out of Peter's mind and focused his thoughts on a pair of facts that carried a clear and menacing *implication*.

What did it was an *emotion*, fear, which he could articulate: "I could lose a client over this!" But an emotion like this doesn't appear alone. It is accompanied by a process of reasoning. Peter knew:

1. Sandra controls Bruce.
2. Bruce controls the company.
3. *Therefore* Sandra controls the company.

He knew this from the start but now he was scared, and fear gives such knowledge a new implication.

His process of reasoning here is less reliable than the one we pulled out of the first scene, and as a guide to action it is weaker. Here's why.

In the first scene it was *true* that the courts have determined that partygivers share the liability of people who drink at their parties and then drive cars. And since the "we" of the conclusion are the partygivers, we share the responsibility for Peter. There is some ambiguity in the term "responsible" but its legal definition has been made clear enough by the courts to serve as a warning to partygivers.

So it's a reliable guide to action. We let Peter drive, we share the risk.

The conclusion reached by the drunken Peter in Scene 2 is weaker as a guide to action because there is more ambiguity in the key verb of the fact pair, the word "control." How far does Sandra's control over Bruce extend? Would she try to dictate his choice of a lawyer?

It is something of a stretch to give the name of "facts" to 1 and 2 in Peter's reasoning. And "control" may not have precisely the same meaning in 2 as in 1. As statements about power relations, 1 and 2 are inherently tentative and slippery—but Peter was a scared man. He had just heard Dave utter the dread sentence, "Sandra is really pissed."

He is menaced by her power, whether he can calibrate it or not. All Dave had to do was remind him that the company would be responsible for his drunk driving, then scare him by telling him that Sandra is pissed, and Peter's nimble mind did the rest: 1, 2, 3, and he caves in.

There's nothing wrong with his reasoning. It's the best he can do in the circumstances. His "facts" are actually probabilities and approximations of the truth, and he knows it. The so-called facts, in other words, don't always have to be true. They need only be probable or indicative, at least in cases like this where there's no prospect of uttering verifiable statements about reality.

There is a kind of reasoning (deduction) in which facts (statements corresponding to an external reality) lead inevitably to true conclusions. But suppose Peter had tried to reason in this airtight way: "I fear I'll lose this client. Why do I fear that? Because Sandra is pissed. O.K. what are the hard facts about—"

He'd quit right then for the simple reason that *there are no hard facts*. There are only approximations, probabilities, and contingencies. If he guesses she actually could get him fired, he still has to guess whether she would. This kind of thinking is a jungle of degrees and possibilities, and the thinker discerns immediately that he cannot find certitude no matter how long he looks. So he falls automatically back on a style of reasoning that takes probabilities as its starting point instead of statements that can be proved.

But the way the fact pairs behave is the same. The probabilities and approximations act like facts. One is not enough. "Sandra controls Bruce" would leave him cold. So would "Bruce controls the company." Unfortunately for Peter the two are a couple and he is forced to consider 1 and 2 together. And when the flash comes he is starting at 3.

In both scenes the listeners changed their minds and took action under the combined influence of emotion and reason. It has been clear since page 1 that emotion plays a critical role in persuasion and now we can see how. Whether the emotion or the reasoning comes first doesn't matter.

Let's take a guess and say emotion comes first. Peter is scared and searches for the reason. He feels menaced by "Sandra is pissed." Naturally he wants to know why. He grabs fact 1. No explanation there, and still he feels this gnawing sense of jeopardy. He grabs fact 2. There's an instant flash of light the moment the two coexist in his mind, and in the flash he sees the cause of his fear: "Sandra controls the company."

In this scenario the mind searched for a rational explanation of the emotion.

Now let's run it from the other direction. Peter listens to Dave's assertion that the company is responsible. Of course he already knew that and he also knows he's drunk. So he knows the conclusion. All this is purely rational.

Next Dave tells him, "Sandra wants me to drive you home."

Now Peter's mind says, "Oh ho, I see it all. She's involving herself in this because of the company—." As he completes this thought he gets the word that Sandra is pissed. Now his reason throws gasoline on the tiny spark this statement would ordinarily produce, and suddenly he agrees to a demand he had refused a minute before.

Whichever comes first, reason or emotion, or if they come crowding in on top of each other, they compound each other, strengthen each other, and create something new.

Sometimes emotion is like smoke. Seeing it we know there must be fire. We search for this cause of our emotion and our reason says, "Yes, right this way," and proceeds to explain the emotion to us.

Fear, hope, desire, and other emotions seek to be justified, and only reason can do it. If it fails, the emotions whimper and die.

And our powers of reasoning leave us cold, unless . . .

Suppose you read that McDonald's stock has multiplied by a factor of X since 1970. You calculate that an investment of $10,000 in that year would yield a fortune today. Quite a number, but it's purely abstract until the phone rings and a voice says: "Hello Ms. Fortunata, this is Gregor Samsa from the law firm of Beetle and Bugsby. It is my sad duty to inform you that your Uncle Jake has assumed room temperature. Poor Jake invested $100,000 in

McDonald's stock in 1970 and . . . but he made some trades . . . and then he bought some . . . and he sold some of his . . . so when you add it up, uhh . . . by the way, you are his sole heir so I wanted to tell you . . . uhh . . ."

Your emotions are now clawing for more facts.

Before we put together a grand strategy of persuasion we should note an interesting fact—not an approximation or probability—a fact. It is that in Scene 2, Dave, the supposed persuader, did not complete the circuit. He didn't even draw the electrodes into proximity. Peter, the listener, did it all.

Dave's big contribution was to remind Peter that the company was responsible for him and then to scare him. Peter did all the intellectual work. Dave was shrewd enough to know that all he had to do was set the juice flowing through circuits that Peter himself designed and built.

FOUNDATIONS OF A PERSUASION STRATEGY

Now let's draw some conclusions of our own.

1. *The arena of persuasion is the mind of the listener.*

We asserted earlier that a persuader is not somebody who gives a speech and flashes a bunch of visuals. A persuader, as Eric Giler argued, is somebody who seeks first of all to know the mind of his listener. We explored this theme in the chapter on audience power. It is now time to add another perspective.

A *listener is powerful because the game is played on his home court.* It is his mind that will receive or reject the evidence the speaker proffers and his mind that will reason upon the evidence.

The power of the fact pair, our dynamic duo, is not only that it leads the mind forward to unexpected conclusions or back from known conclusions to unexpected sources. The power of the dynamic duo is that *it is irresistible.* It is therefore the best way for a speaker to influence events in the mind of the listener.

If you introduce a fact pair and start a process of reasoning running in somebody's mind, *they cannot stop it.* Disagree or disregard it yes; ignore it, no. Peter couldn't stop himself from pulling the two facts close together till they illuminated the conclusion that worked with his fear.

If you tell me something I didn't know, for example that Sandra controls Bruce, and I already knew that Bruce was the CEO, I can't help myself: I have to see that Sandra is a power in the company, or at least could be if she chose. I am launched on the effort now to learn if Sandra's power extends, or if she chooses to extend it, to regulating company affairs. In what sense, to what extent does she control Bruce?

The process of working out the *implications* of the facts and the conclusion goes forward in my mind involuntarily.

If you tell me the baby is in the boat, and I see the boat drifting toward the falls, what else can I do? What can any mind do but conclude that the baby is in danger?

And this conclusion is not some inert glob of informational protoplasm; it's a cry for action. This is the kind of conclusion that makes people jump in the river and swim for the boat.

2. Reason is not sufficient.

There's an old spiritual that sings: "Faith is sufficient." It's instructive that nobody ever sings "Reason is sufficient." It's not.

We know too much. Our minds are stuffed with truths, or propositions we take to be true, supported by good evidence and sound reasoning, and we ignore 99.9% of it. What picks a truth out for notice is that something makes it important. This something is usually an emotion connected to our vital interests or to our sympathy for other creatures, whether standing on two legs or four.

If we're told that a dog has died it may mean next to nothing. All creatures must die. If we are told a dog has been whipped to death something happens to our view of the case. If we are then told that this happened in the next street to ours, the distress intensifies.

And then a neighbor comes in and reports it was our dog, our Rex, Tubby, Juliette, or Moose, and we are lacerated, seared by a "simple" fact.

Not so long ago a learned scientist gave a presentation. He proposed to plant colonies of bacteria in the bodies of sick people, and those creatures in due course would multiply and cure the host body of its ailment in a kind of vaccination process.

A fascinating idea in its way, and the presentation should have been riveting, but in fact it was dull as dust. He didn't connect his idea to the emotions or interests of his audience. He did not, for example, appeal to ambition by exhibiting a viable business opportunity; appeal to the profit instinct by showing convincingly that the scheme would yield a return in less than a decade; or appeal to human sympathy by showing graphically what diseases would be conquered and how.

He offered a thorough and well-reasoned argument and a fair-minded listener could have guessed it was based on sound science and might someday work wonders. But the presentation and the presenter brought no spark to the tinder. Even the driest tinder won't ignite without a spark.

3. *Emotion is not sufficient.*

Calling emotion "coded experience" asserts a fundamental rationality inherent in feelings and urges that are often denigrated as intellectually worthless. Nothing is worthless that arises from experience, except to a person who can't learn from experience. Normal people use emotion in two ways.

First, their emotions store the lessons of experience in the only way they can be stored and still be immediately accessible. We can't keep track of all the facts; our biographies are too long and dense with detail. What we can keep (and quite near the quivering surface of the psyche) is the emotional aftermath of experience.

The restaurant-shy banker is an example. So is anybody who has ever been bitten by a dog. His reaction to a dog running loose in the park will differ from his unbitten brother's.

Likewise if hope runs high in a young woman entrepreneur who has not yet been cut by the sharp edges of life, or in a mature woman encouraged by a steady string of successes, then these two will be influenced by emotion—and ought to be. Even unfounded hope has its utility.

Second, emotion also serves as a smoke signal. Dave started to pay attention when Sandra showed him he had something at stake. Dave then pulled the same trick on Peter, who howled in his mind, "I could lose a client over this!"

These men smelled the smoke and knew there was fire somewhere. So emotional signals urge us to ransack our minds. What we seek is a way to tell *what they mean* and how much weight to assign them.

But emotion alone is not enough. The persuader has to use reason as well. We sometimes smell the smoke and go searching and find there's no fire at all, or one too small to justify the emotion.

Sandra was in a tizzy. Suppose she communicated her anxiety to Dave, sold him on her reasoning, got him all foamed up, and off he runs to stop Peter—and finds that Peter is not so very drunk after all. Peter accounts for his staggering by saying he tripped on a handbag somebody dropped, and that it wasn't he who fell on Bruce but Bruce who fell on him. What happens to this supposedly power-packed emotion now?

It's gone. Emotions seek their own justification in reason. If they cannot find it, they expire or undergo some degree of transformation. So it is folly for a speaker to arouse emotions that lack a rational business justification.

In the absence of a justification it would have been folly for Sandra to scare Dave with "we could lose everything."

What have we been doing in the last few minutes?

We have placed the activities of persuasion in the mind of the listener and shown that the listener takes part in his own persuasion. We have watched persuaders using reason to start up and/or guide the flow of thought in the listeners' minds. And we have noted that persuaders must also use emotion to give the reasoning processes (and their products, the conclusions) personal meaning to the listeners. Neither reason nor emotion alone is sufficient. The listener must *see* and she must also *care*.

It's not enough just to close every circuit on the board. The successful persuader will make the ammeter jump too.

We have recognized that it's not always possible to launch your argument immediately and gain a fair hearing. Often you have to do some introductory work to open the other person's mind. Arguments launched prematurely are like paint applied over chips and rot: wasted.

And we've seen that an argument consists of evidence and reasoning—facts or stuff that somebody uses as facts, together with the attempt to draw their meaning. And we've seen that their meaning, if it's to carry any power, has to be linked to an emotion like hope or fear, something to make it personal to the listener. We found the *meaning* of the facts in the conclusion of a process of reasoning, and we found that listeners (people with minds that won't sit still) sometimes go searching for meaning, spurred by emotions warning them that their self-interest is at stake, even if they don't yet know why.

To complete this scheme all we need do now is add two points.

First, emotions signaling something good do the same work. It doesn't have to be the fear that Peter felt. Feelings of hope, joy, gleeful anticipation, relief, admiration, desire—all these, when aroused by a speaker, also send us searching to learn if there is a structure of evidence and reasoning to justify and further encourage them.

Second, the fact pairs have to form a unity. The statements introduced into evidence, whether voiced or implied, must relate to one another in such a way as to press us to believe a third statement that seems to flow from the first two.

If Dad says, "It's Father's Day," followed by "I'm hungry," we may conclude he wants somebody to take him out to dinner. If he says, "It's Father's Day," and follows up with, "Rex has fleas," he has simply uttered two unrelated statements. These two "facts" are not a dynamic duo. There is no possible conclusion to be inferred from them.

THE STRATEGY OF PERSUASION

From all this we can derive a strategy of persuasion that will guide our efforts at the level of tactics and methods. A strategy must be simply stated and easily grasped, like an elevator pitch. The more complicated the task the simpler the strategy must be.

As for complexity, it's difficult to imagine a more horrific and complex phenomenon than World War II, yet American strategy can be stated easily in a few words:

"Join with Great Britain and the Soviet Union to defeat Germany first. After the victory in Europe shift all power to the Pacific and defeat Japan."

At that same level of simplicity we can formulate a persuasion strategy:

First gain a fair hearing if you can, then present an argument that will stand the test of reason, and touch the audience personally.

With this strategy to guide her a persuader won't get lost in the turmoil of a chaotic meeting. She can always refer to it in her mind and sense its three elements: gaining a hearing, standing the test of reason, and touching the audience where they live.

The three are equally important but in any persuasion attempt it is the argument that must stand the test of reason. How exactly does a listener's reason test a speaker's argument?

THE SKEPTICAL LISTENER

A listener distrustful of your argument will look for weaknesses in one of two places, possibly in both: your facts and your conclusions. If she finds something wrong with the conclusions, she'll then examine your reasoning as well.

This skeptic, especially if she is trained in logic, will understand the *form* of your reasoning. She will recognize your dynamic duo and conclusion as a *syllogism,* and the real skeptic will instantly know when there's something amiss in it. For example:

1. All porpoises are mammals.
2. A reader of this book in New Jersey is a mammal.
3. *Therefore* the reader in New Jersey is a porpoise.

Number 1 is true; 2 could well be true. So it's not enough for the listener to ask whether the "facts" are really facts. She must also look with care at the conclusion. This one is an obvious falsehood but false conclusions are not always so conspicuously false. Nor is it immediately obvious what's wrong with the reasoning here.

What's wrong is that the reasoner has committed the fallacy of the undistributed middle. But there is no need for us to examine fallacies and other aspects of formal logic in any detail. A businessperson doesn't need to carry a textbook of logic in his briefcase any more than a military officer or hospital administrator does. What he or she needs is the kind of testing, critical mind Susan Hammond has.

And the businessperson who seeks to persuade others must be proactive about constructing an argument that a fair-minded but critical thinker like Hammond will approve.

So the critical listener probably is not looking for logical fallacies but she will very probably know when a fallacy (a piece of false reasoning) has been committed. And she will find it out by asking what Susan Hammond asks: Does this make good business sense?

If that sounds too easy, it's not. It would be much easier to test a series of syllogisms against a list of fallacies and give each a "valid" or "invalid" rating. That is a pretty mechanical procedure. But it won't work in business because we do not present our arguments in naked syllogisms.

They are there and we sometimes do make them explicit in our speech and visuals. In fact showing the march of the facts is one of the prime uses of visuals. More often, though, we move too fast to set forth all our premises; and quite often we state the conclusion only and allow the listener to infer the premises.

No conclusion will stand unless supported by premises, but that doesn't mean we have to lay out the whole sequence. What we do need to do, as presenters, is to examine our own conclusions and assertions critically. A quick and efficient way to do this is to take the assertion and see if we can construct a syllogism to support it out of the evidence we have offered (or implied).

And as listeners we gain tremendous potency if we're able to take apart a speaker's stated conclusions in the same way. In so doing we can test his premises for truth or probability and his reasoning for soundness, just as we ought to test our own.

So if, as speakers, we don't express the syllogisms that drive our argument, what do we express? Or, more accurately, if the syllogisms are mostly implicit, what is it that we make explicit? To what do we give the emphasis when we present an argument?

If you listen to good presenters at work, you'll find that they marshal their evidence in waves or stages, and that each stage is flagged with a thesis statement. The stages in turn build up support for a *general thesis*.

The general thesis is the culminating, climactic statement that is supported by the whole argument. It may be stated first or last (more on this later) but in either case it is the statement that everything else points to.

Evidence, reasoning, earlier conclusions, and subordinate thesis statements, all these are deployed for a single reason: to give truth and force to the general thesis.

A thesis is a statement that, if accepted, changes the world for the listener.

And it's the thesis that the critical listener subjects to her most thorough and searching scrutiny. When Susan Hammond asks, "Does it make sense?" the "it" is usually a thesis. And what she means is, "How does this thesis fit into business reality as I understand it?"

What we have to do now is see how the reasoning process known as a syllogism is related to a thesis. A persuader who understands this fit will be equipped to build a formidable argument because she'll be capable of crafting the kind of thesis that a critical thinker will agree to.

THE BUSINESS PLAN AS A LOGICAL INVENTION

Let's approach the question through the medium of a familiar but formulaic invention, the business plan.

Judging by their performance, most speakers who present a business plan think their job is to convey information. The written plan might run twenty to sixty pages, and they have only, say, thirty minutes to present it orally and through visuals, so they cram in as much information as the time will hold.

But this concept of the job can lead to confusion. For example, a speaker who aims simply to convey information can easily fall into the trap called the Chinese Glove Fallacy.

There are a billion Chinese, each having two hands, creating a potential demand for two billion gloves. This kind of statement is often followed by something like: "And all we have to do is capture a measly 1% of the market and we'll generate revenues of $XXX in Year 2."

Certainly the speaker has to demonstrate that a market exists, but his equally essential task is to show that his company can reach and serve it. This cannot be done with evidence alone. It takes logic. Let's try it.

1. They need billions of gloves in China.
2. We make gloves.
3. *Therefore*—what?

Therefore nothing. Numbers 1 and 2 are not a dynamic duo.

The speaker has to create a combination of premises that lead on to a conclusion. He must, in other words, go beyond the presentation of information into the presentation of logic.

Information is not the end, it is the means. The persuasive presenter will use information dynamically to build syllogisms (explicit or implicit), because a syllogism has a conclusion. And conclusions prepare the listeners' minds to accept the subordinate theses and ultimately the general thesis.

In this conception the job of presenting a business plan shifts from conveying information to building a logical structure to win assent to a thesis. It is much more interesting that way. For example:

1. For the first time in history laborers and artisans in China can afford work gloves.
2. Our survey data show a strong desire among workers for the three benefits of work gloves—insulation, protection, and grip.
3. *Therefore* our marketing and sales plan targets workers and emphasizes the three benefits.

■ ■ ■

At any business event a good share of the audience will be wishing they were:

- playing baseball
- listening to music
- cuddling or at least talking with somebody beautiful.

The business speaker has to overcome these fantasies by substituting some amusement that is both possible during working hours and equally or almost equally rewarding. Information won't do it. Information is a box of dead electrodes. Only logic can do it. Our minds have a passion for logic.

Every reader who rejects, embraces, or suspends judgment on the logic of the last couple of pages attests to this assertion. You can do a lot with logic—use it, butcher it, be fooled by it—but the one thing you can't do is ignore it.

A good persuader will take pity on all those listeners who wish they were somewhere else by making it worthwhile to be exactly where they are. He or she will give them logic, and they will eat it up.

THE SUBORDINATE THESIS

We have a question in suspension. How do the syllogism and the thesis relate to one another?

We have just seen an example. We saw a reasoning process in which the thinker took note of a fact, that Chinese workers for the first time can afford to buy work gloves. The speaker then introduced another fact, deriving, presumably, from survey data, that they *desire* three benefits that gloves deliver. If he were speaking with extraordinary care, this thinker would have said, "I conclude that Chinese workers can afford what they want—the benefits cited in our survey data." That is the conclusion of a loose syllogism.

But the speaker, seeing it wasn't necessary to go in baby steps, leapt to, "Our marketing and sales plan targets workers and emphasizes the three benefits." He has not yet stated a thesis but he has taken an indispensable step by drawing a conclusion that will stand in support of one.

Next our speaker might bring in some data or expert opinion on wages and disposable income and link these with the company's estimates of manufacturing and distribution costs, margin requirements and such, and come up with a price point. He is now in a position to draw the conclusion that a significant segment of the market can afford to buy gloves that the company can afford to manufacture and sell at price P.

It'd be tedious to draw out every premise and conclusion but it's clear where all this is leading. At some point, after reaching some preliminary conclusions, the speaker will feel confident about uttering a subordinate thesis such as, "Our sales projections under the conservative scenario show gross revenues of $XXX in Year 1, rising under this marketing plan to $XXXY in Year 2."

This is a thesis in the dictionary sense—a statement to be tested against criticism, an idea to be discussed and proved or disproved. And it qualifies as a thesis under our own definition of a statement that, if accepted, changes the view of the world. As a subordinate thesis, this statement capitalizes on the evidence and reasoning deployed in one specific part of the presentation, the marketing part.

A business plan is an integrated whole, and, as this example shows, marketing cannot be cleanly separated from manufacturing, finance, distribution, and the other parts. But it is possible and indeed necessary in presenting the plan to give distinct treatment to each major segment. The aim is to achieve thematic unity on each part—to address the major questions to be found in each.

A listener who accepts a subordinate thesis as substantially true, true enough to serve as a basis of further reasoning, will perceive the "world" depicted in this part of the business plan in a new light. She or he will think, "O.K. They know their market. They've got a way to reach a segment."

Something has clicked into place. This is just what a subordinate thesis must accomplish. "O.K, I heard the click. Let's go on."

(To clear up a technical point: you could probably call every conclusion a thesis according to the dictionary definition, and that's why our own stipulation of changing the view of the world is needed.)

You will never have time to state every premise, draw every conclusion, transform the conclusions drawn at one level into premises at the next, and so on. And if you had the time you still wouldn't do it because it'd bore you to death.

Only take baby steps when you see that the listener demands it, as Dave did in his dialogue with Sandra. She piled on the evidence precisely because she saw there was a step in her argument that Dave was rejecting.

This isn't to say you should skip the evidence. Skip what you can and keep the argument rolling. Very few in your audience enjoy absorbing raw evidence but practically all enjoy seeing evidence marshaled into marching battalions—so give them what they like, give 'em logic!

A conclusion is a steppingstone: necessary, but not a place you want to pause. It takes evidence (stated or implied) to support a conclusion, and it can then be used as evidence to support another conclusion.

The subordinate thesis plays a higher-order role. It is more than evidence because it crystallizes what's most important in some wave or segment of the presentation. It is what happens when reasoning goes to work on evidence.

It may be useful at this point to remind ourselves that we are talking about how to make a powerful argument. As it happens we have reached the question of how to choose (and write) the most important sentences in the argument, the general thesis.

And let's continue with the business plan as a logical invention because it offers a fair field for choice. From the typical business plan a speaker could write dozens, maybe scores of general theses, depending on the audience. The plan is a gold mine. The thesis you choose to present is the gold.

So let's do two things now. Let's see in a general way how you choose a thesis and then how you structure the argument to give it clarity and force.

CHOOSING THE BIG THESIS

As you would in any presentation, give some thought to who the audience is. Ponder the power-benefit handshake.

If you're presenting to an investor, you need a broad, all-embracing thesis that, when accepted, will declare the company to be a sound investment *for that investor.* What's good for an angel will not be so good for a venture capitalist. And the capitalist in turn is looking for a different deal from the conventional lender, who in fact isn't really an investor.

Or are you presenting the plan to your own team, where your purpose might be to win genuine approval of a new set of performance standards? Obviously you'd need a different general thesis.

Are you addressing a meeting of suppliers interested primarily in long-term reliability? Another thesis still.

Besides the audience you have to consider your own goals. What thesis, when adopted as his own by a listener, will best serve your goals?

The general thesis draws together the major themes and claims set forth in the subordinate theses. It serves your goals by making positive changes in the way this particular audience sees your company and its enterprises. It leads this audience toward the power-benefit handshake. For example:

To suppliers: "In the next two years we will undertake major product line extensions, supported by a growing revenue stream and stronger operations, marketing, promotion, and distribution capabilities."

To venture capitalists: "By Year 3 we will be in a position to make our decision, whether to seek a strategic partner or prepare for an initial public offering."

One way to write the general thesis is to pause and imagine a sentence or two that, if they passed with approval through the listener's mind, would dispose him or her to stand up for the power-benefit handshake. What would be the last thing this powerholder would think before she holds out her hand?

THE FLOW OF THE ARGUMENT

With each segment of the argument the listener should feel that something has been completed; not that there's nothing more to be said, but that he or she has heard enough for the present.

Suppose, for example, that product life span is an issue. In that case you have to face your strengths and weaknesses and assess your chances candidly. Here as elsewhere you have to exhibit Subject

Mastery, Candor, and the other elements of the persuasive persona, and you have to offer a unified, thematically complete presentation of the issue. This of course will include a brief view of the dark side of the moon.

How mature are your products now on the market? What new ones are in design or manufacture? Is the competition catching up?

And somehow in your treatment of this issue you must express a subordinate thesis. For example:

"We are aware that our Silk Bandana security software will be superseded in the near future, but it is still a strong revenue producer. We have a follow-on product in preparation right now, and we are writing marketing materials both for Silk Bandana owners and new customers. We plan to roll out the new product while Silk Bandana is still going strong."

Thematic completeness means addressing the essentials while keeping strictly to the point of that segment of the plan. But for the presentation or argument *as a whole* thematic completeness has a different meaning.

In its overall sense it means putting the whole argument in all its phases at the service of the general thesis. Not that you repeat the general thesis at each stage like a mantra. Definitely not. But the whole of the argument must support the general thesis in this sense:

Every subordinate thesis should incline the mind of the listener toward assent to the general thesis.

This sets you up with what every presenter needs, a simple *organizing principle*. The argument will be appropriate, complete, and powerful if it does this job of supporting the general thesis. No argument can do everything you'd like it to do. A good one organizes itself to do exactly this.

This goal, this rationale, gives you a principle of selection (what to include and exclude) and a test of emphasis (where to put the weight). No rationale can do more.

Whether you state your general thesis first or last is a tactical decision.

First. If you state it at the beginning or even sketch it in a suggestive way, you help the audience follow the argument. They will know where you intend to go and will grasp the relevance of each wave as you pass it before them.

You sacrifice suspense and surprise to gain coherence and clarity in the minds of the listeners. If, as is often the case, you will gain nothing from suspense and surprise anyway, you will want to consider stating your big thesis first, especially if the audience is basically friendly.

If you only suggest it at the start, you can still get the benefits of relevance and coherence, and gain a kick at the end by stating it completely.

Last. If you hold it till the end, you draw the audience wave by wave to an uncertain destination—which is especially effective with a basically hostile or uncommitted audience. Not quite sure where you mean to take them, conscious of a growing momentum and an ever deeper involvement as they assent to one subordinate thesis after another, they probably enjoy the ride more.

The risk is that some listeners may get lost or may miss the significance of some fragments of your argument because they cannot see how they relate to a whole.

Late statement is more dramatic and yields deeper psychic involvement. Early statement yields a stronger sense of how the argument hangs together and reduces the risk of wasting part of the argument.

RAISING THE VOLTAGE

We've been treating persuasive reasoning as if it were a flow of current with the syllogism serving as the switching device—the current flows from the known (the "facts") to the previously unknown or unarticulated (the conclusion). We'll stick with that metaphor while we address the next question: how do you raise the voltage?

We saw two methods in the dockside drama: a) pile on the evidence and b) instill an emotion. There are several other ways, most of them involving strengthening the evidence by making it more comprehensive or clearer. We'll look at only the most important: example, metaphor, analogy, the appeal to authority, and story.

But none of these tactics will seem as strong as they really are unless we first sketch the process of *inductive reasoning*.

You're kidnapped by a flying saucer and dumped in Chemistryville. Hungry, scared, and penniless you wander the streets and alleys of this alien city trying to elude the 'droids in green-and-yellow coveralls. In three encounters the green-and-yellows have beaten you on sight. You are desperately seeking the 'droids in red-and-yellow because one of them smiled at you.

You have, by the all-too-simple process of induction, figured out the best explanation of your immediate danger: green-and-yellows are enemies and red-and-yellows might, just might, be friends.

Your reasoning is not airtight but it's the best you can do on the available evidence.

Your guess about the red-and-yellows is extremely shaky, being based on one instance only. But the guess on the "enemies" feels strong because it's corroborated by an emotion: fear. The very thought of rounding a corner and bumping into a gang of green-and-yellows has got you sweating.

This style of reasoning, called *inference to the best explanation*, is often the only one open to business thinkers. Whether we are persuading, listening, working, deciding, or just observing and holding back, we use this inductive method all the time, not because we prefer it but because we must.

The occasions when an airtight deductive syllogism is available to the business persuader are vanishingly rare. That's why as persuaders and as observers of the evidence we resort to the "syllogism of probability" where probabilities must substitute for facts, and some ambiguity in the meaning of terms has to be tolerated.

In a deductive syllogism the conclusion is said to be "demonstrated" because given true premises the logical thinker *must* move to the conclusion. In inductive reasoning the conclusions are not proved but *implied*, sometimes quite strongly. That's all we can hope for and frequently all we need.

That's how you identify the enemies in Chemistryville. Surely the evidence doesn't prove anything—but it does carry a clear and convincing implication, and if you know what's good for you you'll evade the green-and-yellows till you can get out of town.

Meanwhile back in the real world where people are making deals, seeking jobs, and selling gizmos, *induction is it.*

That's why logicians and engineers both claim it, why dictionaries define it as the process of reasoning from particular facts *that do not cover the case,* but also as the process by which a changing current in a circuit produces an electromagnetic field in a neighboring circuit. Or, in our terms: *crackle, zap, flash!*

Now for a bones-only survey of persuasion tactics that strengthen induction.

Argument by Example

Examples turn the abstract into the concrete and the imaginary into the real. "Courage" is an abstraction, a mere idea, but a girl who mounts her pony immediately after being thrown is an example of *courage in action.* This girl is also a specific kind of example, namely an *exemplar.* An exemplar is a person serving as an example, a role model. When the same girl grows up, faces the stereotypical thinking of prejudiced men, perseveres against it, and does not let it defeat or embitter her but succeeds in spite of it, then she becomes an exemplar.

Examples that illustrate and examples that inspire are both invaluable to the persuader.

The *illustration* makes the "facts" clearer and more lively. "We need somebody around here who isn't afraid of failure. We need the kind of courage that gets right up after a spill, learns the lesson, and starts over again." The speaker of that sentence made her meaning clear by illustrative example.

The role model or exemplar does both jobs, explains and inspires. "No, it won't be easy. Most of our prospects, especially the best ones, are so busy their answering machines have answering machines. But take a look at Emily. What a record!"

Argument by Metaphor

You can also clarify meaning and give life to your argument by using metaphors. When we call Joe a "whirlwind," we are using a metaphor to say in two syllables what might otherwise have required a string of dead words—for example, "Joe works hard every minute and devotes tremendous energy to . . ."

If you explain the word "section" to someone unfamiliar with mechanical drawing by passing a knife through a block of Swiss cheese, the newly exposed, previously concealed surface is a metaphor for the term you seek to explain. It is one thing (which we can see and understand) explaining some other thing that was not readily apparent to the dialogue partner.

And the girl who remounts her pony is herself a metaphor of courage. She is an exemplar *acting out* a specific virtue.

Argument by Analogy

An analog clock is one whose hands move in a way that can be compared to the passage of time. The minute hand moves relatively fast and the hour hand slowly; and the two speeds are comparable to the speed with which the minutes and hours pass. The position of the hands changes with passing time. Digital clocks don't do that. You can't just glance at a digital clock; you have to read it.

That's the utility of an analogy, which is a kind of comparison that sometimes blends into metaphor. When you employ one, your listener can capture your whole idea in a single leap of his mind. "Learning this job is like learning to ride a horse. You're going to be thrown but it won't kill you."

The listener sees the whole idea in one glance—that this job is tough, that spills and setbacks lie ahead, but that skill, patience, perseverance, and maybe some courage will triumph in the end.

There are other nuances and information already implied in the analogy: that learning the job takes time, that it involves mastering something powerful (a set of techniques? a machine or system?) and that it's somehow thrilling or otherwise psychologically satisfying—that a reward of personal pride lies ahead for those who succeed.

That's a pretty prolific message—all of it packed into twenty words. This "packing" is what gives metaphors and analogies their remarkable efficiency and power.

Argument from Authority

When you cite an authority in support of your evidence or thesis, you enlist his or her prestige in your cause. Investment advice from your Uncle Luke might not be worth listening to—till Luke informs you that he's merely paraphrasing a quote from Warren Buffett.

A persuader has to make his own case; no authority can change that; but authorities can be enlisted to strengthen the argument by serving as expert witnesses.

Argument Supported by a Story

Everybody knows the story of the frontier boy who taught himself to read and write by the flickering light of a wood fire while he scratched his letters in charcoal on a shovel. The boy of course was Abraham Lincoln. Writers and teachers have been telling this story for over a century to inspire children—and perhaps adults as well. How does the story do its work?

It works by giving the listener a pattern. We are told the beginning—the poor lad in a dark cabin, sprawled out on the hearth on a winter night, poring over a simple schoolbook and marking out his letters with a scrap of burnt wood. And we know the ending—the boy becomes the man who leads the nation through the supreme crisis of its history; the same man who writes the Gettysburg Address, one of the classics of American literature.

So we as listeners fill in the middle, using facts that we know from Lincoln's life to shape our own contribution to the story. And as we do this we seem to feel the whole significance of Lincoln's personal achievement—how he did with scant advantages what we are asked to do (if we are among the lucky) with more education, more resources, and more help than he ever got.

Thus the story that begins as a fragment becomes a whole, and we seem to see the entire life span of a noble, struggling figure. The story is a form; where we find voids in it we supply them from our imagination. We see—in fact we participate in creating—the meaning of it all.

How These Tactics Work

An *example* gives a concrete instance of an abstract idea and lets the mind see it come to life.

A *metaphor* brings in an image or object that is in some way like the one being discussed, to make it clear and vivid.

An *analogy* compares one event, process, or thing to another, using something familiar to make it easier to understand a new or less familiar idea.

Both metaphor and analogy clarify and vivify a point by showing how something else that is different is also similar.

The *appeal to authority* strengthens the persuader's case with the claim that somebody respected is associated with it—either by agreement or by having something to do with its origin or design. The appeal to authority is especially pertinent when expert knowledge is needed to evaluate the case, because when confronted with a question requiring expertise, we tend to delegate our thinking task to a trusted authority.

A *story* can support an argument in many ways. One is to humanize the characters. Another is to show their affinity with the listener. Most powerfully of all, a story can give coherence and direction to scattered, chaotic evidence.

In his lectures on persuasive speech Adam Smith stressed the power of the story to spread credibility throughout the whole of one's argument. A persuader who tells a coherent story need not prove every element of it. The listener who accepts the major parts will tend to accept the whole story and search it for a relevant meaning.

A story is an attempt to make sense of life by showing how one event follows another and how this sequence is influenced by character. Thus a story told to support an argument can display character and show the march of cause and effect.

So you want the current to go running through your circuits and every once in a while a bulb lights up—that's a subordinate thesis. And you're confident in your ability to encourage in other minds the same kind of flow that's lighting up your own. As each new bulb glows your confidence increases that the general thesis will impress your audience as a new way to see the world you're describing.

This is the ideal. This is what you sweat for. Now let's look at a way to make it happen.

We'll use familiar terminology. Your ultimate persuasion goal is to win assent to your general thesis. And we've already recognized that the subordinate theses are useful precisely because they encourage the listener to assent to the general one. They have a preparatory job to do. So, as we noted a few minutes ago, the parts of the presentation should work together. Whether you present the parts one after another or weave them together, there should be a harmony among them, such that in supporting one another they do their big job of supporting the general thesis.

And if the subordinate theses are going to feel natural and justified to the listener, they have to be supported in their turn by the evidence and reasoning in each of the parts.

Obviously what we've got here is a hierarchy. At the bottom level, "facts" imply conclusions, which in the next round play the role of "facts" to support higher-level conclusions, until at some point you decide that this part of the presentation is ready to be capped with a subordinate thesis. You say it. And now the audience should feel that this segment of the presentation has achieved thematic unity. You are ready, and so are they, to go on.

As you utter each subordinate thesis you move the audience (you hope) closer to a state of readiness to hear and assent to the general thesis. But we are talking about a way to make all this happen. What is it?

It's a thing called the Factor Funnel.

Let's make the assumption that the piece you're working on is a standup presentation and you have time to prepare it. This is good and bad.

The good is that you can do the brain work to get the parade ready. You marshal your waves and plan how you'll march them past the audience echelon by echelon. This lets you do your absolute best to justify your general thesis.

The hard part is that the audience expects nothing less. You can't skate. Even if you're a terrific presenter with talent like Chris Stevens's you dare not try to get by on your acting gift. The reason is simple: they are not dummies. If you charm them and don't present a real argument, your reputation will grow in all the wrong directions.

So do this. Ask yourself: *What is the best way to formulate the subordinate theses?* That process of finding and thinking through the subordinate theses is the key to the composition problem. Here's how the Factor Funnel will help you turn the key.

On the computer or on paper list every factor that influences your thinking on the subject of your presentation. Every one, whether it militates for or against your planned general thesis. (Admit right now that the general thesis may change as you go deeper into preparation.)

A "factor" is any force, fact, myth, prejudice, hope, number, goal—anything that makes a difference in your thinking or the objective situation.

If it's the pricing decision on the new software product, you'd list such factors as the number of people working on the product, rollout date, cost per unit now, cost after so many have been sold, weaknesses of the product against present and future competitors, strengths, competitive pricing, the image effect of high and low prices, attitude of the sales force, implications for marketing and promotion, product life span—

Your list could easily run to twenty, thirty, or fifty factors. That's O.K. Of course you can't work them all into your presentation and you shouldn't try.

An aside: Never feel obligated to cram your whole notebook into your presentation. The notes help you to shape your own thinking. The presentation shapes the audience's.

So you're staring at a bewildering screen telling you you've identified, say, forty-seven factors of all kinds that create this reality called your subject, and shape your thinking about it. Nobody can organize a convincing presentation out of forty-seven pieces, and even if they could, the audience couldn't absorb it.

You'll be tempted to shorten the list. Don't do it. If you can, add to it. Add any item whose addition or subtraction could possibly make a difference in the situation/problem or in your thinking about it.

Your next step if you have time is to retire. Get a cup of coffee, play a round of golf, sleep on it if you can. Whenever possible you should schedule your preparation to allow a night's sleep. Your conscious powers will run at half-speed and low output until your unconscious mind has smoothed the path.

When you return to the list a funny thing will start to happen. Without your having lifted a finger the factors will begin to pull together into affinity groups. As you see this happening in your mind, arrange them in groups on the screen or paper.

The first few will virtually jump to their respective camps. After a while you may have to take some on a tour, showing them the various camps and asking where they feel at home.

Some won't go anywhere. They're misfits. Fine; let them float on the fringes. The important thing is that the others are grouping themselves under themes—the *factors* associate in affinity groups that can be titled with phrases like "elasticity of demand," "competitive advantages," "marketing opportunity," "revenue streams." These are the *themes* that organize the factors into a short list of maybe four to eight, certainly no more.

Now you begin to see the main elements of your show.

The themes, like the chapters of a business plan, ought to cohere. Each one taken singly ought to be a distinct subject within the larger subject of your presentation. And each should give you a chance at thematic unity.

If you present the main elements of each with a sound instinct for what's important and what can be left out, your audience should feel that you've given them all they need, at least for now—that's thematic unity—and that you've given a global presentation of that theme.

Each theme then becomes the basis of a subordinate thesis.

If one of those misfit factors is still swimming around in space and it begins to worry you, maybe it's more important that you realized. There's nothing wrong with moving factors around. Most of them will refuse to budge, they're at home and they know it. But this is the time to experiment. Bring the roving planet into the

Building Up an Argument

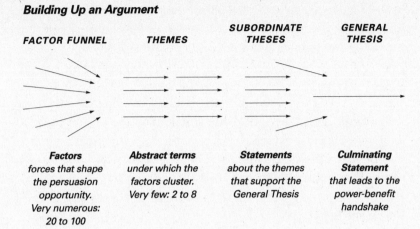

FACTOR FUNNEL	THEMES	SUBORDINATE THESES	GENERAL THESIS
Factors	**Abstract terms**	**Statements**	**Culminating**
forces that shape the persuasion opportunity. Very numerous: 20 to 100	under which the factors cluster. Very few: 2 to 8	about the themes that support the General Thesis	**Statement** that leads to the power-benefit handshake

galaxy and plant it somewhere and see if it stays put. Or is it a synonym for some other factor already safely lodged elsewhere?

The Factor Funnel is a device that creates groupings so easily you won't even feel a strain. And it shows you what ground to grow your subordinate theses in. The factors are the soil and the fertilizer.

See what emerges before you make a writing effort. The best theses jump out at you and bid for your attention, and if somebody asks you, "How'd you think of that?" your likely response will be, "It just popped into my head." This popping is sometimes called "invention."

Even when the idea is there, the actual expression of the subordinate thesis orally or in writing can be tough. It is creative work. It can be effortless or it can be the most demanding part of your preparation task.

If it proves difficult, try speaking it into a tape recorder. Speak as if to an uncommitted but friendly listener and start with, "Would you agree that I have shown that X?" When she says, "X? What is X?" go back to the recorder and say, "X is . . . ," and try to articulate the subordinate thesis. It won't work every time. In speaking and writing nothing does. But it may help you hone your English.

Now with the subordinate theses decorating your screen you can take a critical look at the general thesis you started with—if you had one at all. You can refer back to your goals and forward to the power-benefit handshake, study the subordinate theses, and write your general thesis to do what we saw a general thesis should do: encourage the listener to put out his hand.

VISUALS

Visuals give direct support to the subordinate theses and indirect support to the general thesis.

The best visuals are simple and bold. They convey one idea per frame. They are legible to viewers in the last row.

Simple and Bold

Think of visuals as a mostly blank canvas whose very whiteness serves to guide the eye to the symbols it frames. Those symbols, whether print, drawings, or graphics, must be spare enough to be *comprehensible in a single glance.* If they require sustained reading, they distract the audience from you, the speaker. An audience that is reading visuals cannot listen to the speaker.

If the symbols crowd out the white space, the emphasis is lost and the viewer begins to labor. A crowded frame, especially one that's dense with print, forces the viewer/listener into a reading mode and compromises her listening. She is trying to read the visual text and keep track of the spoken text at the same time.

Probably the worst mistake a speaker can make with his visuals is to display one text on the screen and speak another. Second worst: display a text and edit, cut, or ad lib it orally. The viewer/listener is caught between two texts.

Let the white space occupy almost all of the frame. This virtual blankness is itself a message that the symbols, few and spare as they are, are what's important. Simplicity makes the viewing easy and boldness makes it memorable. Let the boldness be both visual (stark against the background) and intellectual (one clear concept).

For example, if you flash a graphic that shows your stock fund outperforming the S&P 500 by a steadily growing percentage, stick a label in the widening gap that says, "Wide and Getting Wider."

Use words and numbers to the degree necessary and no more.

Visuals are no place for excess. If the data demand it, because what you're presenting is complicated, show your (graphic) evidence in stages and devote a separate frame to your (printed) conclusion. Then if you speak the conclusion as well as display it, make sure your oral and displayed texts are the same.

One way to make your conclusion stick is to show it in print on a visual, darken the screen, move closer to the viewers, and state it with your voice. The shift from a mechanical device (the overhead projector, for example) to a human being with a body and voice can be quite powerful.

The idea is to show it *graphically* in numbers and trend lines, *visually* in print, and then, most dramatically, to move your body closer to *say* it. You darken the screen to deny them a choice. They *must* look at you now, and now is precisely when you want their concentrated attention.

Visuals, in other words, are not an interlude in the drama but a vital part of it. Their chief function should be to clarify meanings so that you as the presenter can, by voice and bodily presence, suggest the importance of those meanings.

Let the simplicity and boldness of your visuals complement the simplicity and boldness of your presentation style. The way you design and use visuals and the way you run the projector are elements of your style.

The overhead projector is one means by which you control the room. Turn it on and the audience expects something easy. Surprise them by making it interesting as well. Show your visuals, then *turn it off*. Now all eyes are on you and the natural expectation is that you are going to do or say something to carry the presentation forward. You have given yourself an opportunity.

Many business presenters keep the screen lit throughout the presentation. Why?

Never let the lighted screen dominate the room. You dominate the room.

One Idea per Frame

A simple, effective use of the overhead projector is to present the members of a team. Let the ones who are present stand as you introduce them. Remember that names can be difficult. If a woman's name sounds like Schultz, it can be spelled several ways. Flash her name and let her stand forward and well to the side, so the eye of the viewer will go to the screen and read the name, then move away from the screen to the woman herself—eyes are always grateful when they're allowed to move from something artificial to a human being.

For team members who are absent, flash a high-quality color photo of the person plus the name in upper- and lowercase letters, which are easier to read than all capitals.

As the picture comes on screen you can say, "This is Bob Jonas. He's often called Jones but Jonas is the name. He's our V.P. for marketing and sales. We wish he could be here today but he's in Los Angeles negotiating a contract with a survey firm."

With Jonas's picture still lit, tell briefly what he brings to the team. Tell one of his major achievements.

The visual shows his name and portrait; you tell his value. Let your respect for Jonas come through.

If you're showing the performance of your fund against the S&P 500 and rivals, do it in stages by using overlays: first the S&P line; then Rival no. 1; then no. 2; then your own line.

One idea per frame builds drama and is more memorable to the viewer than the experience of simply observing the four lines climbing northeast and seeing that yours is on top.

Like any medium of information, visuals convey data. But a visual that also leaves an emotional imprint is a visual that goes *boom*. The one-idea-per-frame approach lets you build a case, or build suspense, and then move to a climax. We're not talking about the sinking of the *Titanic*, just a perceptible click in the listener/viewer's mind as your frames take him or her step by step to clarity and assent.

Legible to People in the Last Row

Think of yourself as a headline writer. You're not writing the news story, just the headline. If the people in the back can't read it, what good is it? A tiny-print visual excludes them and they feel it.

A graph with visible trend lines and illegible numbers on the axes is a frustrating and eventually irritating experience for the viewers in back.

When you flash a visual, you take your audience into a different medium—different from speech. Reading a printed text is not the same as listening to a voice and watching a person as she speaks. The printed text may be compelling but it lacks the speaker's character.

Give them your character, for all the reasons we touched on in Chapter 1. Good visuals help you do this in three ways.

1) They intensify the drama by asking the audience to shift from speaker to symbol and back again. They relieve the eye by offering variety. They can signal the start of a new phase of the show, whether you turn the screen on or off. In either case something new is on the way.

2) They strengthen your facts by making your information graphic. When two trend lines cross or diverge, your visual has conveyed data more dramatically than you ever could with your voice alone.

3) They let you flash a subordinate thesis, if you so choose, in print, to get the sense of it across before you utter it with your voice to give it just the right emphasis.

Visuals can strengthen your premises. This in turn gives weight to your conclusions. And visuals can help you pick your subordinate theses out of the flow, for proper emphasis by voice. All this makes for a stronger argument, with premises conspicuously marked, and thus for a stronger character.

Whether you put your general thesis on a visual too is a delicate question that you can only answer case by case. However you introduce it, be sure it reaches them from *you*. It must proceed straight from the integrity of your whole presentation, as an expression of your individual competence and honesty.

GOAL-ORIENTED IMPROVISATION

Those pesky audiences don't always listen and sometimes won't let a speaker speak. How do you articulate an argument in an out-of-control meeting—when everybody wants his air time and nobody will let anybody else speak for more than a minute? Sometimes the longest "speeches" in meetings like this are mere sound bites lasting ten to thirty seconds.

How, in the midst of such chaos, can you marshal your evidence in smart platoons and march each echelon impressively past the reviewing stand with its banner flying? (That banner is the subordinate thesis.)

Of course you can't. If you try, you risk being marginalized. What do you do?

There is in fact a strategy for such a battle. Let's call it *goal-oriented improvisation.*

An improv artist doesn't show up at the club with a blank mind. He or she has a whole bagful of ideas, many of them worked to perfection in earlier gigs. Likewise a businessperson who hopes to move a meeting in the right direction will come with a full goal bag. She will select her goals according to what's possible in the chaos that unfolds before her. She may even, on carefully chosen occasions, contribute to the chaos to deflect the meeting from a disadvantageous course.

She has a rationale. It is to achieve those of her persuasion and action goals that can be achieved and not to try for too much. If everybody is talking at once it's a sign there's no consensus. Maybe her best persuasion goal is simply to move the group one step toward agreement on a sane agenda for the next meeting.

So let's say she starts with the question: why is everybody talking at once?

The answer will have several parts: ego, ignorance, clashing agendas, laziness, unpreparedness, and so on. But the thread running through the whole tangle is that the group is in a preconsensus stage in its thinking. Our speaker sees this as a stage so early that there's no substantive thesis the group is capable of accepting and not even an argument they are capable of taking in. She defines this condition as an *opportunity.*

Her action goal, let's say, is to get a certain item on the agenda for the next meeting. Ideally this will be one of the subordinate theses of her argument—assuming she has one already outlined in her mind and is only looking for a chance to press it. So she could reason like this:

"I wish they'd spend a few minutes discussing elasticity of demand. Will buyers pay up to the High Price for this software or won't they? Is it good enough? What do we know about their habits that would help us decide?

"I wish we could discuss questions like that instead of interrupting each other every ten seconds!"

Her subordinate thesis is something like: "They *will* pay up, and in sufficient numbers to generate the revenue we need." If she succeeds in getting agreement to discuss this, that will mark the achievement of her action goal. (She may have more than one but let's look at just one.)

What persuasion tactics would move the group toward her action goal?

1) If there seems to be an assumption that they won't pay up, to *plant doubt* about it.

"Hey, guys, not so fast. Everybody said Glass Slipper was overpriced and look what happened." (Speaking time: five seconds.)

2) If nobody has an opinion on demand elasticity, to *introduce it*.

"Isn't it time we faced a question? Will they pay the High Price? Obviously we've got to study that down to the ground before we can even discuss this intelligently." (Speaking time: ten seconds.)

3) If there's a Friendly faction being drowned out by Hostiles, to *rally the troops*.

"I hear Bob, Kathy, and a few others talking what sounds like pretty good sense to me. Bob, it looks like you and I arrived at the same place independently." (Speaking time: ten seconds.)

4) If the discussion is mostly visceral—short on facts—to *advance a premise*.

"Does anybody know how many units we'd have to sell at the High Price to generate as much revenue as the phase-out product generates now? Anybody? I've got some figures on that." (Speaking time: nine seconds.)

5) If the chaos is frustrating everybody, or merely a majority, to *name the pattern*.

"Hey, hey, I love you guys but what's going on here? Is this a meeting or a mob?" (Speaking time: four seconds.)

To be followed as soon as possible by, "Why don't we admit we can't even agree on what to disagree about. Let's define our job as identifying the things we have to talk about tomorrow if we're going to get started on this thing." (Speaking time: ten seconds.)

GUIDED ENERGY

The syllogism is given pride of place in these pages partly for its analytical value. You will seldom reach your conclusions by consciously arranging facts in neat pairs (or strings, if you're working out a polysyllogism); but it will always be possible to reason back from a tentative conclusion to the premises that supposedly justify it.

You find yourself believing something and wanting to assert it in your argument. Test it. Can you formulate premises that would press a reasonable mind to accept it? If you intend to be your own most severe critic, which you should, your best critical tool is the syllogism.

And of course it's equally effective when you find yourself wondering why the other guy's argument sounds a little wobbly. And there's another reason to call attention to this remarkable circuit board. By looking closely at it, as we have, we can see the source of its power.

Here now is the force that drives the syllogism; the same force that can be used to guide a chaotic meeting. Let's call it *implication*.

The difference between an inert fact and a premise is that *a premise is a fact that implies something*. When two or more premises combine to drive our minds to a conclusion, what drives us is the force of implication. The premises taken together imply the conclusion.

Whoever wants proof of this need search no further than his own mind. If I shout: "My God, there's a baby in that boat!" I've said it all. The implication is clear and urgent, provided only that the listener knows the boat is drifting toward the falls. Implication is something we *feel* mentally, a force that seems to reach us from the outside but that we own as soon as we begin to move with it.

We've been playing with the metaphor of the two electrodes and the flash of current leaping the gap. This demonstrates how the syllogism works by showing a familiar phenomenon to help explain an obscure one. It gives a picture we understand and supplies the necessary technical terms—current, circuit, and voltage, for instance.

Now we are ready with a full vocabulary for the reasoning process itself, because now we can give the correct name to the voltage that drives the current through the circuit.

"Current" corresponds to the movement of consciousness over the premises to the conclusion.

"Circuit" corresponds to the pattern of movement—which can be deductive but is far more likely to be inductive.

And "voltage" corresponds to the power some statements have to imply others.

When we name that power—"implication"—we have gone as deep as we can go into the logic of persuasion. Confronted with certain kinds of facts, the mind stops. But there's another kind—the kind that impels us to move forward. These are facts that the mind treats as a kind of lens through which human intelligence sees the hitherto unseen.

There's a whole industry furiously studying the question of how this happens. If the answers to this and associated questions were anything less than mysterious, then all those people holding down university appointments in the "science of mind" would have to find other jobs.

But for the persuasive speaker there's no mystery. He or she must simply recognize two cardinal points:

1. The method is induction.
2. The force is implication.

■ ■ ■

A minute ago our thought-leader said:

"Does anybody know how many units we'd have to sell at the High Price to generate as much revenue as the phase-out product generates now? I've got some figures on that."

This opens the ears of the Neutrals and sets the Hostiles trembling in their boots. There's a whole gestalt implied in what she said that can be set forth as if it were a string of premises. That's exactly what it is:

- The phase-out product is all but obsolete.
- It nonetheless generates revenue stream s on unit sales of n.
- The new product meets all needs met by the old.
- Users need the phase-out product or something that meets the same needs.

Passing these in review, the listener quickly senses an accumulating force of implication. Every statement seems to tilt the mind a certain way. The experience has an identifiable feel to it—less like doing an algebra problem, more like following clues. Not deduction, but induction.

You could almost say, "Demand for software to satisfy customer needs is inelastic."

And if you say it, bingo! You're looking at something like:

1. Demand for the old software has generated revenue stream s on unit sales of n.
2. Demand for the new software will equal or exceed demand for the old (meaning: demand is inelastic).
3. *Therefore* the new product will (or could, absent a competitive surprise) generate revenue stream s or maybe more.

This leaves out production and marketing costs, competitive pressures, and a score of other factors but each of those is another fight. All the speaker is trying to do here is establish that the Higher Price alone is unlikely to depress demand or revenue.

If she can win assent to this (a subordinate thesis), she and her allies will have moved one stage toward consensus around the high price point.

Her reasoning is not immune to challenge. Her subordinate thesis is a thesis in the dictionary sense, a statement to be criticized and tested in argument—which is exactly her persuasion goal, to get that debate started.

■ ■ ■

The most potent sentences in any persuasion drama are the ones that use all the leverage available on those two cardinal points—people reason over business problems inductively, and the force that drives reasoning is implication.

It's not so much what we say. It's what's implied that moves the dialogue. The same applies to our private reasoning—a dialogue with the self, conducted in the theater of the mind.

It follows (these sentences imply) that the most potent sentences a persuader can use are those that are directly relevant and bursting with implication.

Relevant so the listener can fit them into a coherent process of reasoning about one subject. Relevant so that his method of "inference to the best explanation" can go forward. Relevant so he can feel in his bones that he is piecing together a whole argument.

Bursting with implication so he'll feel the momentum.

Of the premises we picked out above, we could say the first one, "The phase-out product is all but obsolete," is weak in implication. By the time you get to "Demand for the new software will equal or exceed demand for the old" you've got a force of implication that's hard to resist.

Your listeners hunger for statements like that, backed by evidence. Those are the sentences that release the energy of logic. Give 'em logic! They'll eat it up.

5

The Pushback Drama —
Resisting and Meeting Resistance

From the beginning this book has proceeded on the axiom that the principles of persuasion are always and everywhere the same.

Whether you're an entrepreneur giving a standup presentation to a venture capitalist, a new hire trying to convince a friend to join the same company, or an executive bringing order to a chaotic meeting, you must still rely on the same "drivers" of persuasion. Every encounter is new and unique, but every one is animated and guided by your persuasive *persona*, your *sensitivity* to the audience and knowledge of its power, your rational choice of *goals*, and your ability to put together a powerful *argument*.

All these show the persuader as creator. But the persuader has another role.

In a business meeting or a chance encounter in a hotel lobby, people don't just stand there, listen respectfully to your argument, and then vote yes or no. They offer ideas of their own. They revise or ignore you. *They resist.*

Most persuasion dramas are fast breaking and out of control most of the time. That is why the fifth driver, which we'll call *pushback*, emphasizes your role as *critic* as well as creator.

It's vital that a businessperson be able to create her own argument. It's equally vital, since her ideas compete with many others, that she be skilled at criticizing other arguments and overcoming resistance to her own.

REAL RESISTANCE, REAL PEOPLE

This chapter opens with true dramas in which businesspeople meet stiff resistance to their messages. The dramas show success and failure and something else that's just as instructive, the attempt to achieve a second-order persuasion goal out of an apparently hopeless case.

A second-order goal is one you settle for when it becomes clear that you can't hit your original goals. The remarkable fact, as we'll see in the first episode, is that a second-order goal can have a higher long-term value than the original.

One word before we start. These scenes will be richer if viewed against the background of an inescapable fact: many persuasion attempts are doomed. The businessperson may have crafted a world-changing thesis and supported it with a dynamite argument; he or she may be the Clark Gable or Marilyn Monroe of persuaders; and the powerholders may be perfectly unconstrained, yet they reject the message and denigrate the persuader as a person.

Imagine a representative of the National Abortion Rights Action League locked in rhetorical combat with a spokesman for the Christian Coalition and you have a pretty good paradigm of the hopeless case.

Yet even then there's something worth fighting for.

When we left Susan Hammond, she was trying to dissuade a client CEO from hiring an expensive and temperamentally unsuitable (from Hammond's viewpoint) consultant to do work Hammond wasn't sure needed to be done in the first place. Hammond was contending that the man couldn't do the work and wouldn't fit into the company culture if he could.

Hammond is not shy about pushing against resistance. When a copy-service vendor named his price for a renewal of his contract she said, "I have some other quotes, so let me tell you my price points. I need this equipment at this price. What can you do to help me?" Then the needle, "I'm trying to keep you as a vendor."

He quoted a better deal and she took it. She called it a win-win deal. (What the copy vendor thought is unknown.) About meeting resistance she says, "Sometimes it's almost coercion."

Once she wanted a bank to consolidate her client company's loans, and the bankers weren't sure it was a good idea. She then pointed out that the bank had just signed a contract with her client for $300,000 worth of professional services.

After laying this down as a fact she interpreted it: to place that kind of faith in the client and then refuse a reasonable request to consolidate loans would be inconsistent. This was one of her examples of urging a listener to consult his or her own idea of what makes "good business sense." Thus she shifts the focus from the small question—whether to consolidate the loans—to the larger one— what kind of relationship do you want to foster with my client? This is a harder, a more "scientific" test for the bankers. It requires them to fit a relatively insignificant decision into a set of more important long-term goals. It's scientific in that it requires the bankers to face a reality they might otherwise have missed: the effect on the client if they should refuse the request.

It is, in short, a reality test. It says that this decision is bigger than you think. The bankers agreed, and the loans were consolidated. Says Hammond, "I try to find a strategy of mutual benefit."

But she doesn't always win.

In the case of the client CEO who was bent on hiring an unsuitable consultant (not competent, too expensive, abrasive personality) she pulled most of her tricks out of the hat, including one that must have seemed very promising at the time—the question: are you trying to get some work done or to build a company? (This usually presents itself in a more familiar form: are you building a product or a company?)

As we saw earlier, she asked another provocative question: If you had all the staff you needed, would this person fit in? This forces the CEO to evaluate the consultant on the basis of his long-term suitability, a harder test than the CEO's short-term need. Presumably if you're "trying to build a company" you wouldn't hire this guy. That at least is Hammond's contention.

It didn't work. The boss was set on hiring the guy and hire him she did. Hammond had lost, the boss won, the consultant started coming to the office every day and Hammond had plenty of time to think about her second-order goals. She had already lost on her original goal of dissuading the boss. What if anything could she salvage out of this?

She never had any doubt about her persuasion technique. It was she who said, "I hate to be told anything. You have to show me."

If Hammond was going to gain a second-order goal, two things had to happen. The consultant would have to screw up and she, Hammond, would have to find a way to let the boss do her own thinking about it.

The consultant did his part handsomely, and Hammond followed a sound strategy. "You have to create a pathway for their mental experience," is how she summarized it.

As the boss began to complain about the consultant's performance Hammond made a set of mental notes. She added nothing of her own. When the right moment came she closeted herself with the boss and said, "Let me feed back to you what you've been saying over the last three weeks."

By reporting the boss's own adverse comments about the consultant Hammond maintained a stance of neutrality while constructing an argument against the boss's hiring decision out of the boss's own mouth.

The boss was big enough to take it—as Hammond had been big enough to take her initial loss. The consultant walked the plank. The company lost some money and gained some wisdom—and Hammond achieved an important goal. "Now when I raise a concern I get a careful hearing."

And this achievement directly served something you might call her mission statement, "I try to leave a lasting impression, for example with a startup, so when I leave it's a sustainable organization. It's better to go one step back if you have to, and really engage their minds."

In this episode Hammond used an initial defeat to gain eventual victory. And what she gained—enhanced credibility and authority—was much more valuable than what she lost.

In this next drama some details have been changed to protect the leading man. Let's call him Harry. His story moves in clearly marked phases: Problem, Decision, Action, and Outcome.

The Problem

Six months into his first professional-level job Harry had reason to be encouraged. He had sold 106% of goal and ranked fourth out of

48 salespeople in the Chicago region. And he felt certain that his customers, makers of injection-molded plastic products, were beginning to value him as a source of information on newly available products and processes.

In fact the only blot on the picture was his memory of the friction that developed between him and his predecessor during the transition. The predecessor would say things like, "You don't have the background," and, "Of course you know you're not going anywhere on this job." Harry would reply: "No, I don't know that."

"By the time he left," Harry said, "we were barely talking."

And it was true that Harry, in his mid-twenties, was inexperienced. But somehow the customers didn't seem to care. He was trying to make up for his weaknesses by hard work and a natural gift for analyzing process problems. If he could get to the factory floor, he could often grasp a problem and propose a reconfiguration based on control devices offered by his company. It was consultative selling and Harry liked it.

But somebody in the Chicago office wasn't impressed, and that somebody was the regional sales manager. Harry had heard rumors that his predecessor, who was respected in Chicago, had "thrown him under the bus."

"That's just hearsay," said Harry. "I don't really know."

But at his six-month review he got a 7 percent bonus instead of the 22 percent promised to all salespeople who hit goal. The next blow was his raise review. They gave him a purely nominal raise and a list of stinging criticisms.

Next came the problem of the free samples. The sales force had been encouraged to pass out samples and Harry grabbed as many as he could for his territory. Then the whole branch exceeded its sample budget and Harry was among those held responsible.

As the months passed the boss came under increasing pressure from his superiors, especially when the branch itself missed goal. Harry was among those who missed his individual goal (by 6 percent for the year) and he felt his share of the unpleasantness passed down the line.

But he had opened thirty-three new accounts that year compared to two by his predecessor the previous year, and he was cultivating some promising new clients, especially one, Mountain Wind, which was poised on the brink of a major expansion.

Harry's record over his first fifteen months was mixed but well above average; and what he couldn't get out of his mind was that the boss had broken his promise on the bonus. His efforts to draw the boss into dialogue got nowhere.

He faced a tough persuasion problem—working in the face of prejudice.

The Decision

Two things happened at once. He saw that he had to make a decision—quit or turn the boss around—and he saw what it was going to be. He remembers saying to himself, "If I leave now, I leave with nothing."

He knew he needed to strengthen his résumé and believed that doubling his predecessor's numbers, which he soon did, would give it a strong opening line, but he wanted something even stronger. And he thought he had it. Mountain Wind's fortunes were on the rise and the people there liked him.

His decision: stay and fight, and make Mountain Wind the pivot of his strategy.

The Action

He had to open the boss's mind and was pretty certain he couldn't do it himself. "What I said wasn't going to make a damn bit of difference. The customers are the ones who count."

So he let the customers speak for him.

The boss knew that Mountain Wind was a potentially huge account, so Harry went to MW and asked his contact there to write a letter. He didn't badmouth his employers. Rather he said that since he was paid by salary and bonuses, not commissions, he'd appreciate it if the contact would write to his boss and comment on one specific aspect of his performance.

Harry did the same with three other customers. Over a period of a few weeks the boss got letters praising Harry on exactly the points on which he'd been criticized in his raise review. Harry was using the review comments as *themes* in his argument (and had he read this book, he might have thought of the letters as subordinate theses).

During those same weeks, when the boss was being bombarded by letters praising Harry on such points as technical ability, product knowledge, and customer relations, Harry himself started leaving messages on the boss's voice mail. If he got a good purchase order he left a message. If a client drew up a specification sheet that contemplated increased purchases in the future, he left a message. These reports would have crossed the boss's desk as paperwork anyway, but maybe the boss would skip over them. By going to a voice medium Harry made it harder for the boss to ignore him.

And at the end of each month he left a longer message, up to five minutes, with a "victory list" highlighting his bigger sales and contacts.

At about this time, with Harry sitting in a customer's office, the customer called the boss and praised Harry. Why do customers do things like this for a new, young salesman?

"I look at what the customer needs," Harry said. "What does this guy's boss want to see at raise time? I look at what affects their take-home pay." Which means solving their machinery and process problems and building a rapport which in some cases blends into friendship.

"I help them out all the time and if I ask for a favor, they're glad to do it."

In the middle of all this, MW called the boss and asked him to finance a trip for Harry to a trade show in New Orleans. Big investors from Hong Kong, the U.K., and France would be there to look at MW's machinery, whose performance and capabilities would influence their decisions about joint ventures. MW wanted Harry to help man their booth, describe what the machines could do, and explain his own company's support capabilities.

And MW made it clear that they didn't want just anybody, they wanted Harry. The boss was incredulous at first but eventually agreed. After the trip came another letter from MW reporting that Harry had helped them land a big deal.

Throughout this campaign Harry never articulated his general thesis. He let it emerge from the argument, and because the boss had to put it together himself it was all the stronger.

The Outcome

Harry continued the campaign for five months—until the boss came through with a solid bonus and then an unscheduled raise plus a few comments like, "You're doing a great job out there." Then and only then Harry throttled back somewhat.

Not unexpectedly, he got a job offer from MW and another from an engineering consultancy. He declined both. He thinks he has a better future with his present employer.

He often hears through back channels that his name is golden in Chicago—all the more since MW started pumping out the big orders he had told the boss to expect.

Harry had been right. He had known that if he could move the boss past his prejudice, his sales figures would speak for themselves. And they did—with a little help from his friends.

Susan Angelastro (Italian for angel star) may have a heavenly name but her basic strategy when she meets resistance is pretty down-to-earth.

"What do I do to get around resistance? I persist."

She proceeded to tell a couple of stories of how she has tried in one case for a year and a half, in another for three years, to set up a meeting with a potential client.

In both cases, she said, "Nada. I'm batting zero."

But she hasn't given up on either one. It isn't against her religion to quit. If a prospect speaks rudely or says a forceful *no*, she crosses him off her list. But until that happens she keeps going back, usually with an average of five calls a year.

Angelastro is an account executive with a big insurance company in its international group program. She sells employee-benefit contracts to U.S. companies with employees working overseas. Companies in Chicago or Minneapolis employing workers in Spain, for example, can buy their health insurance from her.

It might seem that her employer's big name would open doors. In fact she doesn't mention it until late in her initial call. She tries to avoid the effects of stereotypical thinking about insurance sales-people.

She starts with her own name and what she's offering—pooled benefits policies with a cash dividend paid to the buyer at the end of each year.

Listening to her talk about her work, you begin to see that there's more to her technique than mere persistence.

Everybody she talks to is busy (one man has been too busy to see her for two and a half years), so she adapts her tactics to their needs. She is brief and to the point.

"I plant a seed and let it germinate."

When to Pull Back
If they resist, she pulls back, knowing that clients with real needs will remember her when the right moment comes.

"If they say no"—which most do—"I call again in a month or so."

She manages to work into the conversation that her company and its overseas partners know the market in every country where the client has operations, and she emphasizes that the pool contracts she sells pay cash dividends.

As many as five in twenty-five prospects agree to a meeting. As for the rest, "I try to let it roll off my back." But where there's the faintest glimmer of promise she keeps trying. And when they agree to a meeting she follows the oldest and plainest of all persuasion strategies.

"You've got to be yourself. I think people for the most part are pretty smart. They can tell if somebody's B.S.-ing. I think they can always tell.

"You have to gain their trust; you have to make it safe for that other person."

She recognizes that her competitors are offering services not very different from her own. This puts the premium on the character of the speaker. Harry had to find advocates to speak for him. Angelastro must speak for herself.

"Why do they gravitate to me? It's how I present myself at the meeting. The more comfortable they feel with you the more they're going to trust you."

So how does she manage to make this "comfort" happen?

She spends some time (not too much) on casual talk. "But you have to know when to make the pitch. Then you see a blank look on their faces and it's obvious they don't know what's going on. So stop—listen. I guess it comes down to knowing your audience and being able to size them up.

"I might draw in another client or prospect and say, 'I've had clients with the same reservations you've got.' I try to let them know they're not alone by drawing on the experience of others."

But reading your audience, she continued, isn't always easy. She met with a chemical manufacturer in the Midwest and she remembers that in the middle of their dialogue she thought, "I can't read this guy." He wrapped up the meeting by saying, "I can't make any promises."

She let the man alone, and a few months later he called with a question about a country where his firm had a manufacturing operation. She helped him, and he soon signed on as a client. She attributes this success to her self-presentation.

True, she has sincerity and honesty written all over her face, an advantage that not everybody who's sincere and honest has. But one senses that she made a decision early on, perhaps at the very start of her career, that being who she was was O.K. Perhaps too many of us try to be somebody else who we think is better than we are, a star of some kind.

Whether this woman is an angel I won't venture to guess, but by being herself she has certainly become a star in her field.

This next piece could be called "The Education of Corey Darling." He starts as a young man who'd rather hit back than push back, and as he grows a little older and wiser he learns that tough doesn't necessarily mean angry.

And he learns something just as important. He learns that pushback is something friends can do to each other—must do—and still remain friends.

A Guy Who Didn't Pay by the Rate Card

"This was about ten years ago," said Darling. "I was representing a radio station, selling $50 ads, and I called on a car dealer and gave him my rate card.

"He took it and right in front of me he crumpled it up and threw it in the trash and said, 'I don't pay by the rate card.'

"He'd stopped communication. He'd said, 'You will simply take the order or not.' Not very fruitful. What I did was, I left that office—this was in Buffalo—and went to another dealership and I didn't pull out a rate card. I told him I'd sell him all the inventory he could buy at half price, because I wanted him to kill the other guy."

The station went along with the price cuts in its "inventory" (ad time), and the second dealer got the "biggest possible noise at the lowest possible price." The first guy got canned (Darling doesn't know why) and Darling brooded on the incident till a lesson emerged.

If he had it to do over again, "I'd say, 'O.K., it seems you have a price objection here. Can you help me define the problem?'"

Now when he meets resistance—"I keep talking till they don't let me talk anymore, but I'm not selling, I'm asking, 'What kind of availability do you have? What's your price structure? What's the pressure on your inventory? What's your golf handicap?'"

As the questions show, he's not selling $50 ads any more. He's an affiliate relations executive with CRN International, a vendor of radio programming that also buys ad time. Thus he is both seller and buyer.

And he lives by the lesson of that little scene in Buffalo.

"Successful salespeople learn, 'This has absolutely nothing to do with me, nothing at all.' I don't get discouraged, I really don't." And he doesn't get mad. After about a dozen rebuffs, he says, "You hit a point beyond which you say, 'I don't feel shamed, I don't feel humiliated, this is a setback and that's all it is. Where are we going next?'"

He now operates in a nationwide universe of perhaps two thousand decision-makers. His clients are names like Perrier and Campbell's, and the dollar figures are what you'd expect at that level.

But the fundamentals of the game are the same. When he represents the ad buyer, he tries to get the biggest noise for the smallest dollar. When he's selling his company's programming, he's looking at the other end of the equation—but it's more complicated than that. He explains:

"The radio station is a consumer of programming. They can't produce it all. So they're going to buy my programming—hit records, a half-hour cooking show, a call-in show—and we say, 'Take this, and we'll buy back from you some of your commercial inventory'—ad time. That's what they sell. In Boston for example it could be $500 a minute, $1,000 a minute.

"At this level everybody has manners but you still have to push back firmly. Even if the ratings are perfect, I still have to be careful not to pay too much because they want to extract as many dollars as they can and I have to extract all the value I can for the dollar I spend."

So, for example, when Perrier wants to gear up for the hot summer season in the South, Darling sells regionwide programming such as the "Perrier Cool Sounds Report," a concert-listing segment, and buys back ad time for Perrier.

In these negotiations each party has needs, and the players not only know each other, each knows what the other's needs are. The relationships shape themselves for present and future use.

"You're in the game, you made it, and they know you're going to be around."

So when he encounters resistance, instead of trying to "kill the guy" as he did in Buffalo, Darling tries to find out what's going on. "I may not know at the beginning why he's resisting. Suppose it looks like a good mix but it's still not working. Maybe I'm asking for too much. He might say, 'I can't give you that much inventory.'" In other words what looked at first like a price objection might actually be a shortage of inventory.

Darling finds out things like this by structuring his pushback as questions. The lesson might be summarized as: don't fight; ask questions. Then use the answers to move the prospect in your direction.

These dramas can generate a lot of personal pressure. The numbers are big and the career stakes high. It's imperative to nurture the relationship for just that reason. Skipping to a different client, Darling told how this is done.

Suppose he's been through a pretty difficult pushback session with the representative of a group of radio stations in the Midwest. The relationship is frazzled but still intact—at least he hopes so.

Then he gets a call from this very person, and her message is loud and clear. A winter storm is coming to her area and she's sitting on a pile of unsold ad time. Darling gets the hint and says, "I want Campbell's Soup in there." (Cold weather sells buckets of soup.) The rep says, "That'll be a thousand a spot." Darling says, in so many words, "It's worth it, I'll take 'em."

"This is a reward system," Darling says. "I'm rewarding radio stations that worked with me successfully earlier in the year. It's a follow-on to a pushback, to nurture the relationship. I play ball with you. You play ball with me."

There's something noteworthy about Darling's style that doesn't make it over the printed page but bears directly on pushback success. He's very quick and can think around the corner—but his conversations are punctuated by silences, sometimes long ones. He's listening.

You can't push back—from either end of a thesis—unless you know what you're pushing against. And you can't adopt what's good in the other guy's position unless you understand it.

She says it with an involuntary laugh, but she does say it, "I persuaded him with the force of my personality." Anybody who's had contact with that personality will believe her.

The speaker in this, our last pushback story, is Shannon Gilligan, founder, president, software designer, writer, and producer at Spark Interactive, Inc., a Santa Fe–based production company that makes interactive entertainments, mostly murder mysteries. Gilligan's productions, beginning with "Who Killed Sam Rupert?" allow the viewer to visit the crime scene, interrogate suspects and witnesses, and solve the mystery.

The persuasion job she was talking about was obtaining production money for "Sam Rupert." She was at a trade show in California when she saw a video embedded in a game. She said to a publisher, a man she had met once or twice before, "That's what gets me really excited. That's what I want to do."

More specifically she wanted to produce "virtual murders" in which the viewer could play detective—but detectives have to be able to interview witnesses and suspects. This was 1991, and the technology to make that possible within the game format was only just being developed.

Gilligan said, "I'll do everything myself. It won't cost much."

Her hope was that the technology would be improved as her project developed. The publisher shared her hope. He gave her $25,000 and she set to work.

The technology did get better, and Gilligan took advantage of it in "Sam Rupert." Five years later "Sam" had sold over $2 million at wholesale and Gilligan had produced six more interactive murders—the most recent ones on production budgets of about $400,000 each. Her company employed from ten to forty people during this period, depending on need, and Gilligan formulated her own definition of management.

"Essentially it's persuading people that your ideas are worth following through on—whether they're ideas about the organizational structure or creative ideas.

"Management is persuading people to understand your point of view, so they will intuitively and naturally understand what their role is. Then all the energy comes through on the project."

Persuading by Enthusiasm

"The key is enthusiasm. I was enthusiastic early about the possibilities of an interactive story viewed on a computer, and that enthusiasm was communicated immediately, right across the board."

Her concept is a very personal one. She tries to "align" herself with the dialogue partner. "When you've got this tremendous enthusiasm, you're trying to align yourself to that other person's energy so you'll be able to say the things they need to hear to be able to feel the way you do about your project."

This goes for the money-raising phase, recruiting talent, running the company, getting programmers to try what they believe to be impossible—the whole range of persuasion tasks that she faces in producing mysteries. And since each person is an individual she tries to see what they need—broad conceptual strokes or the minute details.

"So it's a matter of tuning in to what they want."

Keeping the Vision

But there's a hazard. In "aligning"—in exposing her enthusiasm and passion—she would sometimes empathize so completely with dialogue partners that their objections began to feel as if they came from her.

"You really make yourself vulnerable. I sometimes found I didn't protect myself from the other viewpoint. You've got to know where the line is—where you're right.

"There can be an almost mystical level or quality, because in a sense you're really aligning your energy field with this other person's and trying to create forward motion.

"Sometimes people would criticize and I was so aligned with them that I would be vulnerable to the criticism. As I got more skillful I'd be able to put up an invisible wall and say, 'That person's got a point but I don't agree and that kind of thinking is not going to get this project accomplished.'"

Gilligan says she had to learn the hard way to keep her vision and (in our terms) still reach the power-benefit handshake.

The Integrity of Her Vision

With Gilligan's story we reach one of the subtlest problems raised by pushback encounters—how to keep the integrity of your vision in a power-sharing linkup.

If Gilligan had commanded unlimited resources—capital, a publishing company, marketing apparatus, and all the rest—she might have delayed her moment of truth till her products reached the market. As it was, she met it earlier.

Murders tend to be messy, yet Gilligan abhors violence. With her characteristic cheerfulness she says her feelings about violence seemed to be at odds with her gift for creating suspense. Publishers need suspense and other story values, and in today's market it's all but impossible to depict a sanitary, bloodless murder and make it believable. And believability is another story value.

What did she do?

"I have softened that antiviolence principle somewhat." She looks at the whole story, the whole thing as a work of art in which violence may have a proper place.

Gilligan alone knows how this "softening" of a principle made her feel, but listening to her talking about it, one senses that it didn't diminish her enthusiasm or seriously cloud her vision.

There must be a balance somewhere between the writer-producer's creative vision and the need to communicate that vision in all its vividness to a paying audience. Gilligan's style of persuading through enthusiasm and reaching the handshake by "aligning" with the other person are her methods of striking the balance.

PUSHBACK TACTICS

Stories like these and scores of others each of us could cite from daily experience show businesspeople pushing back in a variety of situations.

Whether the drama opens with you in the role of speaker or listener, you'll probably be doing two things at once after you enter the dialogue phase—reinforcing your own argument and pushing back against somebody else's. This can be a friendly kind of dance or a bitterly adversarial contest.

Just as a military tactician wants to know the various maneuvers available to him before the battle starts, so the business persuader will build self-confidence and the capacity for quick action by gaining a thorough familiarity with elementary pushback tactics.

Often when a listener resists your argument it's because he's already committed to some other one. In those cases *you may have to rebut an argument he has neither stated nor acknowledged*—one that is only implied by his resistance signals. Or, if he has openly espoused a rival thesis, you may have to weaken it in order to convert him or to show uncommitted spectators that it's not as good as it seems.

Whether your goal is to win over a dialogue partner or to impress some other segment of a splintered audience, *you have to undermine the rival thesis.* Here are some ways to do it.

Test His "Facts"

So long as you maintain in your mind and manner the distinction between your dialogue partner (a person) and his evidence (his "facts") there's no reason why you shouldn't subject his evidence to the severest kind of test. The man or woman is your colleague, customer, investor, friend. As such he or she deserves to be treated with the humane respect we all hope to meet from those we associate with in business. But the facts enjoy no such privilege.

We may understand perfectly why the banker entertains an unacknowledged prejudice against restaurant loans, and we may and should empathize with him as a person. But that's no reason to respect the prejudice or to accept as true assertions that we know to be false or shaky.

If you reason back from the prejudice—the conclusion that restaurants are unusually risky—you inevitably come up against the supposed fact that they have a high failure rate. What this rate is, precisely, the banker is not saying and maybe doesn't know.

To undermine his conclusion, focus on this "fact," the failure rate. If it turns out that it's not so bad, the prejudice stands exposed—that is, the conclusion is unmasked as a mere prejudice.

In fact there are Dun & Bradstreet data showing that restaurants have a lower-than-average failure rate. Merely by citing the figures you bring the prejudice out into the open and make the stage ready for an examination of it. The banker may well say, "I know all about that and I still say they're too risky." That's his privilege. But at least the discussion can now proceed to uncover his real concerns.

And maybe on the other hand he'll listen to a question: What kind of businesses do you support? If he then names a few, any one of which has a higher failure rate than restaurants—and something like half will—you're making progress. His case is falling apart because his key "fact" has failed the rationality test. He may still refuse you but he'll have to find another reason.

Testing the facts is what Dave did in his first dockside exchange with Sandra. She stated that Peter was drunk. Dave tried to refute this by feeding her the answers Peter gave to his questions. But of course his questions were too soft. Sandra easily passed the test when she piled on new facts, and Dave had to agree that Peter was too drunk to drive.

To succeed in undermining a conclusion by testing facts you have to test the *right* facts. Those are the ones in the chain of reasoning that support the conclusion you are challenging. They are the facts that imply the conclusion. They are facts deployed as premises.

Test Her Reasoning

There are two ways to test somebody's reasoning. One is to agree to her facts and then show that her conclusion doesn't follow.

Susan Hammond used this method when she argued to her client's banker that he should consolidate the loans. There wasn't any disagreement about the existing notes or their terms. What Hammond said rather was that given the trust and goodwill implied in the recently signed contract for $300,000 worth of professional services to be rendered to the bank by her client, it would be inconsistent to refuse the consolidation request.

The banker could well have defended his reasoning. In fact, he pondered what Hammond said and agreed with her.

Harry used the same tactic in countering his boss's prejudice. He never disputed that he was young and inexperienced. Nor did the boss dispute his sales and new-accounts figures. What Harry's whole campaign implied was that this set of facts did not support the boss's hostile attitude and paltry raises. The boss at length agreed.

As his campaign continued Harry moved to the other method of testing reasoning, which is to introduce a *different set of facts* to serve as the basis of reasoning.

During the five months of his campaign he was constantly tossing new evidence onto the scales until the boss had to acquiesce and use the new fact set in place of the old. Rather than premises about Harry's inexperience, the predecessor's negative evaluation, and the downside of his performance, the boss at length agreed to base his reasoning on current figures and positive customer testimony. The new fact set, of course, yielded a new conclusion.

Something similar happened in the roundtable discussion about pricing the new software product. The talk is going along without any consideration of a critical factor—customer payback. At the tactical moment a speaker throws this factor on the table and it immediately takes on the status of a premise—a fact that implies something. It cannot be dismissed because it shapes the reasoning that follows.

"Reasoning" means not just how we use our facts but what facts we use. Choosing the facts takes wisdom. Thus arguments over reasoning often come down to arguments over the premises that are the basis of the reasoning.

That's why in an earlier chapter we stressed the need to control the terms of the discussion; terms shape our thinking about "facts."

That's also why pattern recognition is so important. The "pattern" of the facts is nothing more nor less than our way of making sense of them.

Reverse the Facts

Reversing the facts is a way to highlight the contrast between two situations. You admit one fact set and then show its opposite.

"Yes, of course, you can do it that way. You can try to find an insurer in Spain who you know and trust. You can ask him all about health and hospitalization plans offered by companies licensed to sell insurance in Spain. And if you don't feel 100 percent comfortable with the answers or the rates or the terms of the contract, you can find somebody else and start the process all over again.

"Or you can talk to me. You know my company and its reputation, which goes back a century. We have already done all the work and cemented partnerships with the most trustworthy insurers in Spain, on the most favorable terms."

Reversing the facts can also take another form—reversing the positions of the players. It can be very ticklish because it tends toward an argument *against the person* instead of against his position.

"You promised a 22 percent bonus and you gave me 7 percent. Cool. How would you feel if I gave you one third of the work I promised?"

This example shows how crazy you have to be to use the role-reversal tactic but it also shows the possible psychological effect of calling the listener's attention to his or her role. This will come up again in a minute.

"I'm Trying to Follow You But . . ."

If you encounter resistance to your thesis but the reasons seem vague or incoherent, it may be an opportunity to weaken other positions and strengthen your own. You could say, "Wait. We've got so many ideas wiggling around on the table that I'm not sure where it all leads.

"Bob is worried that investing in gold is out of synch with our purpose as a club. Karen thinks that speculating in commodities, even with as little as 5 percent of our assets, is lunacy for amateurs like us. Sally shudders at the very idea of a real estate investment trust committed to properties we've never seen in cities we seldom visit.

"I just don't know where all this takes us. That's why I like a simple, clean, familiar strategy: buy and hold big-company stocks."

Here the speaker's emphasis is on the untidiness of the other positions *taken as a group*. He finds it easier to undermine them as a group than individually. To be honest with his fellow investors he will have to propose, somewhere along the line, a comparison of his idea with others on a one-to-one basis. But the usefulness of his calling attention to the chaos of the group's discussion is that it is likely to shorten the list of options and move his up.

He is on surer ground, both intellectually and ethically, if he can discover the same kind of disorder—too many premises, internal contradictions—in a single opposing position.

What this speaker is saying is that if a colloquy seems disorderly and overextended, it's not conducive to sound thinking, it's inchoate.

Arguing against one policy—seeking to weaken one rival thesis—he might say:

"I agree with Jack up to a point. We certainly ought to look at the gold option. But what do we expect to get out of gold? If it's a hedge against inflation, we'd better be aware that gold prices fluctuate with a rhythm all their own and don't necessarily counterbalance the consumer price index.

"If it's long-term security for our money, we'd better ask how long long-term is. Years? Decades? If it's something of real value to sell off in the event of a general collapse, we'd better ask how likely we think that event really is.

"I'm sorry, gang, I just don't follow the reasoning. I want to make some money on the next upswing. Not next decade—next year. And I'd settle for any time earlier."

Extend the Principle

If you can discover the principle at the center of a rival thesis, it sometimes pays to extend it into the future, to exhibit its logical consequences.

"I get it. You're saying it's management's prerogative to pay a goal-hitter 7 percent when he was promised 22 percent. Management can't operate effectively if it's hands are tied by old promises.

"Let's look at the effects of that. How is the sales force supposed to know when a goal is a goal? Where does their incentive come from? Who are they going to trust?

"And what about new hires? How long is it going to take for the word to get around that promises made on hiring are a dead letter six months later?"

Reverse the Principle

"Of course you've got a point. Management has to be able to adjust compensation in accordance with available resources. Conditions change. 'That was then, this is now.' There's an important principle at stake. But isn't there another one even more important? I think there is.

"If we adopt the principle that management will always keep its promises, then it seems to me that two good effects flow from that. One is that managers will be self-disciplined about the promises they make. The other is that the sales force will trust its managers.

"For both managers and salespeople, then, incentives will be realistic and they'll be real. In that situation too, the sales force will be more understanding when the company hits lean times and has to slow the pace of compensation growth, or even cut back. There'll be a whole different psychology."

Name the Job

This is the tactic Susan Hammond employed when trying to block the hiring of the consultant. Somebody in Hammond's position might say, "You're hiring him to clear this work off your desk. I suggest you define your task differently. Hire him or decide not to hire him as if your job were to build this company.

"We can surely find somebody to do the work. But it isn't so easy to build a cohesive team that will be the nucleus of an entire staff as the company grows."

Name the Role

Naming the role is like naming the job, but it focuses on the individual.

"I can understand why you want to hire him. You see all this work piling up and you're convinced he can do it. That's a legitimate approach but to me it looks like a supervisor's approach.

"What if you saw yourself as a leader? Supervisors properly focus on clearing the work, but leaders have larger responsibilities and approach decisions differently. As a leader you've got to look over the horizon.

"And, too, leaders are responsible to the teams they have already assembled. The teams expect the leader to bring on new people who meet the same standards they did when they were hired."

Telling somebody what his or her role ought to be is obviously a delicate proposition. It can raise tensions and anger. But if you do it right, you can open new perspectives for the audience.

Change the Terms of Debate

This one is familiar; and it's related to the last two. It requires listeners to see the subject with new eyes. "I'm sorry but I just don't see it as you do. You're treating this as if it were a budgetary question. But I see it as a question of company ethics. Do we keep our promises to successful salespeople or don't we? I'd hate to think what kind of company we'd become if we made policy on the basis of this decision."

Exhaust the Possibilities

Assuming you and the audience agree on action goals it can be very effective to show that your way is the only way to achieve them.

"We agreed when we organized that we wanted to achieve moderate gains at moderate risk. So what are we doing talking about apartment buildings in Houston? And gold? We might as well speculate in pork bellies. And the Big Smiles Mutual Fund—all of it invested in China? Are we nuts?

"With the market skyrocketing there's plenty of risk of a correction. So for my money, big-company stocks are the best and safest way to achieve our goals.

"We don't have to look for sleeping giants. We can look for growth opportunities. I'm just saying, let's look in the right category."

Try Analogy and Metaphor

In the last chapter we saw how analogies and metaphors can help build a case. They're just as effective in a pushback drama.

Two famous examples come from American politics.

Democrats are always accusing Republicans of favoring the rich, and Republicans have an answer ready. Here's what they *don't* say: "If we improve conditions for the creative entrepreneur and the job-building company, we will inevitably benefit the wage-earner." No. That's a mouthful and makes a lousy sound-bite. What they say is: "A rising tide lifts all boats." This is quick, it's vivid, and it catches the imagination.

There's another metaphorical response, less well known, and this time it's the Democrats who throw the metaphor at the Republicans. The two parties are in their usual tussle, and the Republicans have just made their usual claim that benefits granted at the top trickle down to the lower orders. At this point the Democrats say, "Right. And if you were a farmer, you'd feed the birds by giving oats to the horses."

Skillfully deployed, any of these tactics can blow a hole in the other guy's argument. But like all powerful weapons they have to be used with precision and care. The proper object isn't to humiliate and destroy the dialogue partner but to win her over.

Rational persuasion goals seldom contemplate the total destruction of the rival position, let alone the rival person. Rather the aim is to salvage what's good from the other side and incorporate it into your own agenda. You want the other person to assent to your thesis because you recognize she too has something good to offer. People work in teams for that very reason.

Problems are identified, priorities set, decisions made, and policies formulated by people working together. The process is what the Greeks called a dialectic and we call give and take.

Scott Barnum, president and chief operating officer of Pete's Brewing Co., sees a trend away from "the boss said it, it must be right" to a more collaborative management style in American business.

Barnum worked in marketing, both stateside and overseas, for Pepsico before joining Miller Brewing as brand manager for the company's beers. Later Miller made him general manager of its American Specialty and Craft Beer affiliates, where he created alliances between small brewers (like Wisconsin's Leinenkugel) and Miller.

At the moment when he had just left Big Beer and was moving to the presidency at Pete's, the upstart brewer of Pete's Wicked and other craft beers, Barnum was doing some thinking about what he sees as the new, developing management style. He begins with two perceptions — "that there's always a *variety of interests* that need to be represented in management decisions and that *authority is less sacrosanct* that it once was."

Barnum said the new, less reverential attitude toward authority has grown more pronounced during his own career (he's forty). Authority doesn't come with the title. "It has to be earned. And it's earned through making tough calls and having them come out right, and *by supporting others.*"

We put that last clause in italics because it's the bridge between Barnum's two perceptions. Good managers seek a variety of interests and viewpoints, and they foster an attitude of collaboration among them and between the manager and the representatives of the various functions and interests.

"Every day you run into differences, and to coexist requires collaboration." This is not the same as compromise. Compromise means the sacrifice of part of the compromiser's aims. This of course may happen, but collaboration has an entirely different feel to it. It means, literally, "working together."

"Often," Barnum continues, "if there's disagreement, companies don't tend to say no. Instead they say, 'O.K., we heard you,' and unless you continue to push you won't get that outright *no.* The companies don't want confrontation.

"It's up to the individual to persist, if he believes he has good grounds, but in general it's been my experience at Miller and Pepsico that it's incumbent on the parties to collaborate. And collaboration takes time and work. This is becoming more and more true in today's business climate where there's a variety of interests and where authority is not so sacrosanct."

What encourages collaboration? Open communication and trust. "It's giving everybody access to all the information. And the more you trust people and open up to them from the start, the better."

A decision process begins with problem definition. This too is done collaboratively. "It's a matter of getting consensus on what the problem is, on problem definition, getting it on the table, and letting people agree or modify the definition."

The idea is to create a sense of ownership in the process of agreeing on a true (useful) definition. Then, "O.K., we all agree now, this is the problem. What are the alternatives? Can we get more information? Now let's look at the implications, the risks."

So the team views the problem from every angle, and the only idea that's untouchable is that the team members' input is valued. Once the decision is made, the next step is to gain acknowledgment of it. This is a new phase in the ownership concept. "It helps create an environment where you get fewer objections and more positive input"—ideas you can use.

Barnum believes that employees are more skeptical of management decisions today and more willing to push back—"and there's more genuine listening by management. So where it's working the climate is less adversarial but at the same time people are more apt to challenge what they hear."

Isn't it risky to push back when the pushee is the boss?

"Actually in some environments when you challenge, you're rewarded." The best companies, large and small, Barnum thinks, are coming to realize something important about decision-making.

"They're finding they can have healthy discussion and useful pushback when people are encouraged to give their ideas. Teams are better organized and there's more cross-functional collaboration than ever."

He has observed that in meetings where the marketing rep used to be the "authoritative leader" he or she is now more likely to serve as facilitator, to draw out the best ideas and see what develops from the clash and competition.

In crises companies often have to act fast and decisions have to be dictated, but a well-led company will follow up with efforts to get people to buy in after the fact. You can't do this very often, Barnum thinks, "because Americans by nature are not lemmings."

"Everybody likes good leadership but people expect to be treated well, to be heard, valued, and validated. In early-stage companies where that entrepreneurial will, passion, and drive are still at work, it can still be 'my way or the highway.' But in later stages you start to evolve to a more team-driven and collaborative environment as opposed to a benevolent dictatorship."

It may appear that the environment Barnum describes is one where persuasion skills fade away from lack of use—where such qualities as cheerfulness, patience, goodwill, and willingness to compromise are the leading traits of the successful persona. But a closer look will reveal a rather different picture.

What happens when "authority is less sacrosanct"? When the boss isn't interested in hearing Yes because Yes tells him nothing? What happens, in short, when freedom breaks out?

What happens is that you get that process called a dialectic, which is nothing less than a free clash and competition of ideas. It's no accident that this trend should show itself at this point in history. Barnum in fact attributes the atmosphere of freedom in business decision-making to the spread of the free market worldwide and to the consequent intensification of competition. Ideas, like products, are tested from the outset against the toughest and the best. "Good enough" isn't good enough any more.

And what kind of person is likely to emerge as reliable and effective in this brave new world? Barnum said authority has to be earned. But that statement doesn't apply to the boss only, its effect ripples out and down and applies in varying degrees to everybody.

So what kind of person will succeed? Obviously the kind who advances the best ideas and advocates them most persuasively. Or:

1) the leaders will be people who choose the right action goals, promoted by the right persuasion goals, and

2) they will be people who win assent to theses that support their action goals.

To put it succinctly: they will be people who *project a persuasive persona* consisting of Subject Mastery, Ability, Empathy, Candor, and Steadiness.

It is people like these who stimulate and guide teams, who best represent them in cross-functional meetings, who sell their idea products inside and outside the organization, and who are best at all the other entrepreneurial tasks that turn ideas into realities.

In a bureaucratized, command-guided organization the persuasive person can never flourish because such an organization abhors pushback. Such organizations are ruled by Yes and C.Y.A. But in the free market of ideas these three-letter terms have no value. When ideas clash, it is good ideas and good advocates that win.

Who do you want on your team? The answer is the same from Miller Brewing to Pete's Brewing to the small companies that hire people like Susan Hammond.

Pushback dramas are always unpredictable and sometimes chaotic. The chaos perhaps originates in their divided nature; they are part collaboration, as Barnum indicated, but the other part is a contest. Yes, people want to work together, but they're also proprietary and competitive. And if they weren't, there'd be very little push to the pushback.

You advance a thesis. She seems to agree but when she summarizes your argument it turns out she's revised it. You push back, she pushes back, then a third party chimes in with yet another idea and both of you push back against him. He, the third party, vehemently pushes against both of you, at which point a fourth speaker jumps in.

There can be no generic game plan for a contest like this, but a few bold maxims make it easier to hold a true course through the storm.

Maxim 1: Define Yourself

Often there's a huge, sometimes a ridiculous gap between who you are and who they think you are.

You signal agreement on one little piece of evidence and suddenly you're treated like a trusted ally. You pointedly reject somebody's dubious facts and they act as if you had desecrated their mother's grave.

Don't let people define you; define yourself. Do it with your steady character and in terms of your goals, your thesis, and your constituency.

1) *Goals.* Why are you there? Why should you speak instead of remaining silent? *What's at stake* for you, your career, your company?

We define ourselves as actors in the world partly by what we do, partly by what we want to do. A person who keeps both in mind is less likely to lose his head in the smoke of battle. In fact one good

definition of losing your head is losing track of your best goals.
Therefore stay goal-driven throughout the episode, no matter how
stormy it gets.

2) *Thesis.* The thesis is an instrument to serve your goals. By
articulating it (or powerfully implying it, as Harry did) you declare
who you are and what you stand for. By communicating your passions, as Shannon Gilligan does, you also communicate a clear
definition of yourself—and the thesis then serves two purposes: it
prepares the listener for the handshake and it strengthens your character as a persuader.

Nobody has got everything figured out in advance, so it's often
advisable and necessary to revise your thesis in the clash of ideas.
But this is best done in tandem with a reexamination of your goals.
The two influences, goals and thesis, should modulate one another
so that changes in either or both are never recklessly made and are
always done for good reason.

Two good reasons are to accommodate new data or to serve
higher goals that preserve the spirit of your originals.

Changing your thesis is a risky exercise, precisely because it's part
of your identity. Go easy.

3) *Constituency.* The worst fear many people have as they step
into the chaos is that they'll forget themselves—forget who they are
supposed to be. What if I let the side down?

The best way to guard against the missteps that come with such
forgetting is to keep one's constituency ever in mind.

Who am I here to represent? *To whom am I answerable?* Who
will be watching my performance with the keenest eye and the
strongest faith?

A speaker who keeps faith with those he represents will have no
trouble keeping faith with himself.

Maxim 2: Time Your Moves

If the thing you're in the middle of is a real dialectic—a process
where ideas clash to winnow evidence and advance taut reasoning—then it's likely that everybody has something to offer. There are
no empty heads.

Some people will commit themselves early, to push the dialectic the way they want it to go. Others will await the moment of exhaustion, the moment when some idea has worn itself out, in order to turn the meeting to their advantage. And some will pick the moment offering what seems to be the greatest tactical advantage, regardless of whether it comes early or late.

That's three strategies: early, for initial influence; late, to exploit a moment of poise; and whenever the opportunity shows itself.

None is best. All three work, depending on the speaker's talent and opportunities. The essential thing is to recognize that others need to speak. It's a fine art, giving them a chance to contribute yet taking advantage of one's own chances.

Maxim 3: Give Credit

There was a pulp fiction writer in Europe in the nineteenth century who sold story ideas to other hacks. For the price of a lunch he'd sell the outline of a story. When somebody asked him whether he wasn't throwing away his own chance, he said, "No. The more ideas I give away the more I have."

Some people are that way about giving credit. So long as they make contributions of their own (a necessary condition) they gain credit for themselves by giving it to others. For example:

"Clearly what we're doing is trying to improve Jerry's idea. I do think improvements are possible, but let's say it right now, we owe the idea to Jerry. Thanks, Jere!" (Jerry, of course, might welcome the improvements, but don't count on it.)

Maxim 4: Hold on to That Definition

Just as you have to define yourself against others who want to define you, so you may have to define what's going on.

There will be people who will try to transform a dialectic into a negotiation. But the process Barnum described is not a division of benefits or a search for compromise. It is much closer to the architect Jim Groom's "best idea wins." It is a winnowing, criticizing, and creating process in which the most conspicuous contributors will be the thought-leaders, not the conciliators.

Negotiation has an important role to play in business, but a negotiation, whatever else it may be, is no dialectic.

In Barnum's clash of ideas the participants do not judge the outcome by who got what. They didn't come to the table to swap sacrifices and benefits. They came to contribute, and the winner is the company.

And in a well-led company the contributors will get the credit they deserve.

Maxim 5: Be of Good Cheer

Early in this book we quoted John Pope of Reader's Digest on his use of humor in persuasion. We didn't try then and won't try now to search out the elements of how to be funny. There is no point in analyzing it.

But this is the moment to observe that humor's cousin, *good cheer,* is absolutely essential in pushback dramas. The reason is simple.

Pushbacks, which are properly contests of ideas, all too easily become clashes of personality. When that happens, nobody wins and the dialectical process, which is nothing less than Groom's search for the best idea, can suffer irreparable damage.

So a strict separation of the person from the idea is incumbent on every speaker who ventures to criticize somebody's idea. Without real pushback there is no dialectic. But without this separation there's no hope of maintaining the atmosphere of objectivity and civility that is the necessary condition of real pushback.

A man many would call the greatest lawyer in all history, the Roman advocate Cicero, said that the best persuader is a virtuous man of goodwill. Let's cut Cicero some slack on gender sensitivity and agree that the best persuader is a person of sound character who is of good cheer because good cheer is the evidence she gives that she's motivated by goodwill.

In the pushback this translates as follows: the best persuader/thought-leader is one who genuinely wants the best idea to emerge, who gives credit to others, who contributes intellectually with ideas and rigorous criticism—and who contributes morally by brightening the scene with goodwill and good cheer.

RELAY COMMUNICATION

Another kind of resistance, different from all the rest, arises from the structure of a certain kind of persuasion drama. We've touched on it before; it is the relay problem.

You need a bank loan and the only person who'll talk to you is a loan officer who lacks the authority to approve it. There's a committee somewhere behind him that is the real powerholder. The figure on the following page displays the problem and its potential for mischief.

We've already seen that the key to the conundrum is to turn the loan officer into your advocate before the committee. Once again, easier said than done. But the figure helps by separating the problem into its parts.

You address your Message to the loan officer, the Primary Audience ("primary" standing for first chronologically, not necessarily first in importance—but maybe that too). As you recognize from the start, this person is also your Channel to the Secondary Audience, the powerholders.

But no channel is a clear channel; even pure water bends the image of a stick. In addition to all the normal kinds of resistance we've been examining, the Channel may be clogged with "static"— extraneous interference such as mental distraction, fatigue, nervousness, he's too busy, he's getting a divorce, his boss flogs him. This sort of thing is covered by the word "static" in the figure. So your Channel may be a most unreliable medium of communication. Still it's the only one you've got.

And this man, being both an Audience and a Channel, is a power to contend with.

Therefore the problems of Relay Communication are three: to win the Primary Audience, to preserve the Message intact as it travels down the Channel, and to win the Secondary Audience as well.

With the three problems or goals in mind, let's take a closer look at the figure.

The arrows represent your Message or Messages. They also represent movement. So the figure purports to show your Message *mov-*

Relay Communication

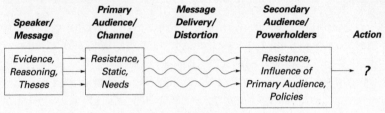

| Speaker/
Message | Primary
Audience/
Channel | Message
Delivery/
Distortion | Secondary
Audience/
Powerholders | Action |

Evidence, Reasoning, Theses → Resistance, Static, Needs 〰〰〰 Resistance, Influence of Primary Audience, Policies → **?**

Did the theses survive?

ing. What makes it move? Where does the motive power come from?

Initially from you. From your personal drive, passion, and concentration; from the persona you project to your Primary Audience. But there's another energy source and it's your logic. We have seen that logic is the movement of the mind over evidence to conclusions. If you can pass the logic through the Primary Audience, it will provide energy to help carry the Message to the powerholders.

So there are two things (and only two things) you can do to reach the powerholders: inspire the Primary Audience and extend your logic.

The bad part about the figure is it makes a human drama seem abstract. The good part is it shows the elements, and here the critical thing it shows, balancing the loan officer's resistance, is the element of his Need. This guy is a banker, imbued with all the appropriate thoroughness and caution, but he's also a salesman.

Like a state trooper, he's an authority figure, but where would the trooper be if he never wrote any speeding tickets? Where would your Primary Audience/Channel be if he never wrote any loans?

So let's follow Harry's lead and think of what the banker needs. Like almost everybody else, he's got a boss. What does he need to show the boss at evaluation time? A folder full of loans that make money for the bank at reasonable risk. And that's how he spends his days, compiling that folder.

You can help him. And help yourself. When you prepare for your meeting with him, try to imagine his meeting with the committee. What you want to see is that moment when he pulls your file out of the stack, pauses to look around the table, and says:

"My next one is an application for a $125,000 three-year note to help a young woman start a dress shop on Zinger Street."

What will he say next? How about:

"She impressed me as a competent, feet-on-the-ground business-woman with a flair for fashion and the experience, knowledge, and personality to make a go of it—and she's willing to mortgage her condo."

If you can give him what he needs, chances are he'll give you what you need.

And the Secondary Audience, the powerholders, have needs too, which are detailed in their policies—as noted in the figure. Your presentation to the Primary Audience therefore should:

- inspire him to be your advocate
- give him what he will need when he meets the committee by keying your presentation to their policies, and
- extend your logic all the way across the figure.

You can best do this last one by reducing your basic steps to graphics and text and providing the loan officer with a packet for each committee member. The packet should set forth your themes and your critical subordinate theses as well as your general thesis.

You can do this in simple outline form—don't be too elaborate. You need not present all themes and all subordinate theses. Present only what's essential and eye-catching.

But in any event, one of the themes should be you—you as the competent "feet-on-the-ground" businesswoman the loan officer believes you are.

There's a lesson in this figure: if you can inspire the Primary Audience, and if your logic is powerful, you can march right through the Channel.

This fictitious case is similar to Susan Angelastro's real cases. She too has to inspire a Primary Audience, and she does it through the impression she conveys of feet-on-the-ground competence. To this, by means of gifts from the gods and by the natural virtues of honesty and goodwill, she adds the kind of personality a benefits-buyer would be happy to work with.

Then she offers sound business logic. She supplies her contacts with the kind of essential information that extends the logic of her proposals to the next higher echelon in the buying company.

In short, she solves the three problems and achieves the three goals of relay communication. She inspires the Primary Audience to be her advocate, preserves her message intact through the Channel, and wins the Secondary Audience too. Not always, but often enough.

6

A Stake Through
the Heart of Fear

A young woman favored by the gods in every possible way—gifted with brains, beauty, success, and the promise of ever more success ahead—stands to deliver her segment of a team presentation of a business plan at the Harvard Business School.

She smiles at the audience of fifteen peer critics, men and women she knows well, and launches into her presentation. In mid-sentence she stops, stares at the audience as if they had turned into wild animals, and spins around. For a dread thirty seconds she hasn't got a word to say.

Another MBA candidate takes the baton from a teammate and speaks a clear, well-formed sentence. He pauses. He speaks again, but it's the same sentence. He does it again—word for word. He looks at the lighted screen, at the chalkboards, and at his teammates seated in the front row. They stare back helplessly. He stands there paralyzed and says the same sentence again.

A man of sixty with *forty-five years' experience* acting, speaking, and teaching before audiences of all sizes raises his hand to make a comment at a meeting of businesspeople, many of whom know him and like him. The moderator nods and invites him to speak. He begins. His tongue clogs his speech, his lips droop like rubber, his hands tremble. Worse yet, he makes no sense. Whatever he intended to say has flown out of his head and all that's left is gibberish.

Some vampires suck the blood of their victims but this one sucks their brains. He heaves carcasses right and left into the ravines of Transylvania, where they land in trembling heaps, sweating, mortified, and incoherent, cursing their tormentor and themselves, desperate for a chance to show they really can "do it" but secretly afraid that the next attempt will end in the same kind of idiotic display of their shortcomings.

The euphemism is "performance anxiety." The real word is Fear, and sometimes Terror.

This is a vampire with an undiscriminating appetite. Old brains, young brains, technical brains, poetic brains, fresh brains, and exhausted brains—he craves them all.

One man I know says there's only one way to meet him, and that's "with all guns blazing." Others say, "Channel it, use it, ride it"—as if fear were a kind of wild stallion. There's merit in both strategies and we'll explore both.

First we need to call on experience to see what fear can do and to note the mistakes people make that open the door to fear. Later we'll sharpen an oaken stake cut from a mountainside tree in Transylvania, grab a sledgehammer forged by the troll of the hill, and drive death through the heart of this freak.

THIS IS NO JOKE

When a victim does a damage assessment after a vampire attack, he sees something remarkable. The damage extends across the body-mind dividing line. This is the vampire's trademark, this broad-spectrum damage.

You get the impression—such are his powers that he could cut off the victim's right leg if he wanted to. Instead he spreads his effects throughout body and mind as if boasting about how versatile and ubiquitous he can be. He can:

- Thicken the tongue
- Distort the lips
- Scramble the bowels
- Set butterflies and bluebirds loose in the stomach
- Make the extremities and limbs feel like taffy and shake like a Model-T
- Erase the memory
- Stifle the voice

- Smother the mind
- Annihilate identity (the "out-of-body experience")
- Knock his victims clean out (although fainting is rare it's quite impressive when it happens)

And these are just a few of his powers. He can do more serious damage by *intimidating his victims* so they never speak at all and thus lose opportunities that might never come again. He can *obsess his prey* so all they think about is him; then they lose track of the drama and pop up with inappropriate remarks, something that might have been just right five minutes ago. And he can inflict what is perhaps the most debilitating injury of all, *irrational humiliation*, the conviction that you're out of your class. "I'm no good at this and I'd best crawl into a hole and eat chocolate till I get a chance to sneak away and bury my miserable self in oblivion."

If you look at the list something interesting begins to happen. You begin to see that some of the effects ascribed to the vampire might have other causes. A lapse of memory can be the effect of fear, yes, but the trouble *might* be that the speaker has overstuffed his brain by trying to memorize his presentation. (If you slip off a memorized track, you're lost.) He might be unable to speak because he's not sure what to say. He might faint from a biologically caused drop in blood pressure.

If we are to conquer the vampire, then, let's start by recognizing both his strengths and his limitations. He is terrifying, for sure, but like a terrorist who takes "credit" for a bomb he never set, maybe the vampire isn't quite so potent as he wants us to believe.

And since we're trying to balance our appreciation of his powers, let's recall that a vampire is not Superman. Superman can hurl the devil clear across Colorado, bounce him off the Rockies, and split a coconut over his head. Vampires can't do that.

Vampires have their little weaknesses. For one thing they always appear in the same black suit and cape, which is very boring. You can spot one a mile away. And they can't do anything at all in broad daylight. Let in some sun and you'll never again have a vampire problem. And of course they are terrified of crosses, so maybe some-how the speaker's *belief* makes a vampire cringe.

And, oddly, they cast no reflection in a mirror. So maybe—what?

These will be our themes; the reader will spot them weaving through the rest of this chapter.

1. You can always tell a vampire
2. They are helpless in the light of day
3. They cringe before a cross—suddenly it's the terrorist who's terrified—and
4. Whatever else he can do, a vampire can't throw his image to a mirror.

ONE SPEAKER'S METHOD

A woman who grew to adulthood in the '50s said that women in her generation were expected to conceal their thoughts and show their legs. She became a painter, mother, and housewife. She marched against the Vietnam War but otherwise took no part in public or business affairs.

With women's liberation and consciousness-raising she started to change and sometime in the '70s decided to step out of the home and into the House. She ran for the House of Representatives in her state and won, the first member of her party ever to capture that seat. The very night they counted the votes she caught sight of the evil freak in the black cloak lurking close enough to send tremors through her body.

Talking to farmers in their barns during the campaign and meet-ing people in public buildings and stores was one thing. She had campaigned mostly one to one, and an audience of one or a dozen didn't scare her. She had some fear trouble with larger crowds and TV cameras, but she had made it through the campaign without a major vampire attack.

But on victory night it suddenly struck her that she was going to have to stand up in the Legislature and talk!

She had one advantage. She knew her enemy. She also knew how to deal with him. How?

"Notes," she said.

She knew exactly what was going to happen when she stood for the first time to address the Legislature. Her mind was going to shut down. The vampire had handled her roughly once or twice in her life and she knew he'd do it again.

"My mind would go blank. Complete shutdown."

She determined she could beat the devil with knowledge, and to make that knowledge accessible she would write simple notes on 3 × 5 cards. She chose cards because they don't shake as conspicuously as paper.

Her cards did shake. The demon almost got her. But an incredible thing happened when she made her first speech on the floor of the House. "They listened!" she says, still showing the amazement of it twenty years later. "They started disagreeing with me!"

For one who had been conditioned to believe that her thoughts were of no interest to anybody this was a sweet victory in itself. And it came to her the moment she summoned the will to defy the vampire.

Let "notes" stand for thorough preparation and you have the essence of the legislator's way of wrestling the vampire down.

Some people are struck with the trembles, some with incoherence, some with selective memory loss. Her fear was total shutdown—and still is, if she is called on to speak without preparation.

So it was logical that she should fill her primary need, which was to prepare a sequence of ideas and write the ideas or topics down on cards. Not the text—that would be too much. Some speakers do write out the text ahead of time—to call up the vocabulary and create the metaphors that will give life and concreteness to the presentation. But the legislator followed a different method, one that I prefer and that I advise most clients to use.

Her method was to work out the best sequence of ideas, then practice the presentation to herself, both aloud and mentally—without trying to settle on one "final" or "best" text. By this discipline she gained familiarity with the material, experimented with her language and metaphors, and grew in confidence. She had no fear of memory loss because she'd written the topics on her cards.

Just the topics. If her preparation is thorough and she designs visuals to present the quantitative data, the rest of the text flows into her consciousness the moment she clicks on the topics.

Most minds work that way, which is why the best notes are simple. We usually don't need text, just the sequence of topics. A written text is a standing invitation to read—and reading a presentation in a business setting is seldom the best way to project a strong persona. A well-prepared mind can improvise text. This is what John Pope of Reader's Digest means by "improvising along well-prepared lines." You get both structure and spontaneity.

So the legislator's note cards showed a sequence of topics—and the cards incidentally solved the problem of what to do with her hands. It is of course best—most impressive—to speak without notes at all, and those who can do it should. But the cards detract very little from one's image, and they are better than risking shutdown.

RE-ENTER CHRIS STEVENS

Let's move now to a speaker who never had a serious fear problem, Chris Stevens. If a woman who lives in fear of total shutdown finds safety in preparation, what does an ace like Stevens do? Does he say, "Hey, fear, get outta here!" Does this fearless speaker regard fear as somebody else's problem?

Not exactly. In fact his strategy is remarkably similar and perhaps more elaborate than the legislator's.

He prepares as thoroughly as possible. "I'm ready for anything," he says. He studies the subject down to the ground. (He's the panelist who knew the brewer's business plan backwards and forwards and also visited the brewery and talked to the staff.)

He imagines hostile listeners and questions. He works out a plan to contend with a lousy sound system. He imagines himself saying something stupid and then dreams up a self-deprecating one-liner that he keeps in reserve.

He gives his presentation minute-to-minute interest and overall direction. And he starts with some kind of display of humor and good cheer that relaxes the audience and incidentally chases away the vampire. Often he asks the audience to be satisfied with a mediocre presentation, because he's so inexperienced (a tactic dating back to Cicero, who died in 43 B.C.).

Neither Stevens nor the legislator makes the Big Mistake, which is to ignore the lurking figure in the black cape. They both respect him.

You can spot him a mile away—if you're looking. And for one who isn't looking, who is perfectly satisfied that he can always perform at the top of his style, there's only one question: *Why?* Why should you think it's *easy* to construct an argument, project your persona, clarify your goals, assess your audience, lead a group's search for the best idea? This is easy? No sir, this is nothing less than a striving after excellence in an art form, and the day that's easy is the day we'll all be issued ten thousand shares of McDonald's stock backdated to 1970.

The businessperson who says, "I'm tops. I'm cool. I've got nothing to fear," is either kidding himself or coasting. Sure, a person who doesn't try needn't fear failure. And one who strives *on every occasion* to improve herself might indeed fail. It is this person, this man or woman who invests effort and pride, who *might* fail. Striving after excellence as a speaker and persuader puts you at risk of an encounter with the brainsucker. You *are* at risk. Experience lets you grow and shrinks the vampire, but experience can be a long time coming.

Get all the experience you can. There is no better way to fortify yourself against his sallies. But what can you do now?

First, preparation. Total Subject Mastery; site reconnaissance; rehearsal to, but not beyond, the point where spontaneity begins to drop; physical prep including adequate sleep and avoiding foods that dry your mouth (coffee) or make you clear your throat too much (dairy products). Audience analysis, goal study, and all the rest.

But there's another dimension, almost another reality that a speaker should explore in the strategy of defeating the vampire. Exploring it, we'll find a way to let in more light—and Mr. Fear can't live in the light.

Preparation is knowledge and knowledge lights up the mind. But Subject Mastery is not enough.

KNOW YOUR ENEMY

If fear were a personal adversary, we'd study his every move and build an FBI-style psychological profile of him. One thing we'd be certain to do is study his strengths and weaknesses. We'd consider ourselves lucky if we could find a clue to his basic strategy. We know what he does, but how does he do it?

If we knew in advance his concept of the operation, we could easily beat him to the objective. If the Trojans had known what was inside that huge wooden horse the Greeks left at the gate, they never would have dragged it inside their city wall, where it disgorged its commandos. They would have burned it.

As it happens the vampire does behave like a personal adversary. His intelligence is excellent. He knows your weaknesses. His timing is perfect. He is malicious. He attacks at some of the most important moments of your career. This is for sure, he knows *you* down to the ground.

So let's just search for that clue. What does he do to his victims that lays bare his underlying mode of operation?

Going back over the list of what he can do, nothing is more striking and strange than the out-of-body effect. This is least likely to hit when the speaker is in dialogue, most likely when the setting is formal and dozens, scores, or hundreds of faces are staring at you and expecting (apparently) something extraordinary. Why else should they sit in silence and let you do all the talking?

Most people who have given a formal presentation to a big audience are familiar with the syndrome. You're in the middle of your argument and all's well. The audience may be a little hard to read but at least some of them are paying attention. Then for no apparent reason you lose track of time.

All sense of the occasion deserts you. You lose contact with the speaker, who is supposed to be somebody you know pretty well.

It doesn't feel as if it's you who's talking. Rather the feeling is one of separation from this talking, walking, gesturing personage who's wearing your clothes. In an earlier chapter we saw that the big fear of a speaker suffering out-of-body syndrome is that he or she will say something stupid, use the F-word, break out laughing, or ask an astounded audience, "Do you really want to listen to this stuff?"

That these horrors seldom occur is no comfort to the separated personality because the real pain of the syndrome isn't what the speaker might do, but the feeling of being out of contact and control. "Is that me? Do I know what I'm saying? Do I know what to say next? If it's not me, who is it? If it is, why am I standing here looking at him?"

VAMPIRE STRATEGY

So let's ask two questions. What is the vampire doing to us and why is he doing it?

It seems he is dividing the consciousness of the speaker. By insinuating himself into the speaker's mind he is opening a chasm between one part of consciousness and another. On this point expert analysis is probably less useful than the plain report of experience. Whatever a psychologist might say about it, the speaker who actually experiences out-of-body syndrome knows exactly what's going on.

His or her "real" self has been divided from the speaking self and the divider is fear. Maybe it's just too scary to inhabit the brain of the speaker, so the "real" self, which is where the fear attacks, has jumped off the train.

Why would a personal adversary do this? Why would this powerful enemy scare your "real" self so badly that it temporarily abandons the other part of you—the part that, after all, keeps on talking and showing visuals and so forth? Here we get into metaphysics, but if you continue with the metaphor of the vampire, of fear as a personal adversary, it's pretty obvious. He does it this way because he is weak. He has to divide your mind in order to have any hope of conquering. What he's afraid of is the integrated personality—the whole, complete, and *united* self. He can't overpower it.

If that sounds too optimistic and poetic, think of it this way. Fear can *enter* your mind but not shut it down. You still know your premises and argument. You still know how your themes coordinate with their subordinate theses and how these support your general thesis. You still know your persuasion goals and how they will lead toward the action goal of the power-benefit handshake.

How do you know you know all this? For the simple reason that the automaton who is giving your presentation is actually giving it. He or she usually does a pretty fair job, in spite of the out-of-control feeling. Even though fear has wormed his way inside, he can't put out the light of preparation. He's afraid to touch the switch.

No, preparation is not enough to keep him out entirely. It *is* enough to limit his effect.

The vampire's strategy is to get in and do as much damage as he can against a well-prepared speaker by dividing her or his mind—by taking over part of the organism even if he can't shut the whole place down. A speaker experiencing out-of-body syndrome is scared, but not to the point of shutdown.

The out-of-body syndrome shows how strong the vampire is, and how weak, and how to send him squeaking back to his coffin.

We already know that Subject Mastery is one of his major bugaboos. The legislator and Chris Stevens say so, and their experience bears them out. The structure of the syndrome shows it too. A speaker who's well enough prepared to continue presenting her argument in spite of fear has got to be somebody who knows her stuff pretty well.

She is, after all, still making sense. The vampire wants to reduce her to silence or to senseless, desperate, mechanical repetition, but he can't. *The prepared mind is one of his big bugaboos.*

What's the other one? The out-of-body business strongly suggests that if the speaker could reintegrate her personality, Mr. Fear would be squeezed clear out. His skinny, crooked little form with all his black capes and baggy pants would go flapping off to wherever he came from and leave the speaker free to do her job.

He divides to conquer but what if he couldn't divide? There'd be no out-of-body syndrome. There'd be no thickening of the tongue, no rubberizing of the lips, no bluebirds and buzzards in the stomach.

Because all these manifestations of fear, from acute nervousness all across the spectrum to complete shutdown, are so many kinds of *interference.* The fear-struck speaker is somebody who's being interfered with. Interference can be thought of as fear injecting itself into the mind to disrupt normal operations.

Even when fear is "reasonable" (because the stakes are high) it doesn't follow that it's also reasonable for our faculties to shut down or our lips turn to rubber. Those effects of fear simply increase our chances of failure. There is no sense in which fear can be both rational and disabling.

No, Mr. Fear is an interferer who seeks to divide us from ourselves and separate us from our natural abilities. It might therefore seem that concentration is the answer. The speaker should perhaps fold ever deeper into herself, concentrate the way Olympic gymnasts do, to exclude all that's foreign and distracting.

This is an appealing idea but it takes the speaker in exactly the wrong direction—as we'll see in a few minutes.

The important thing now is that we know Mr. Fear's weakness. He needs an opening. You can see this every time you watch a speaker who has been nervous and scared throughout his prepared presentation suddenly return to normal the moment he shifts from the speech to Q&A. He's human again. Same subject, same audience, *same stakes*, but his fear vanishes. This is an extraordinary transformation.

So what's going on?

Our metaphor seems to be telling us that the man giving a speech looks like a victim to the vampire but the same man a moment later engaging in dialogue does not. Or at least not so much. Or the speechmaker has somehow left himself open to a brain-sucking attack while the same man a second later is immune or nearly so.

From the vampire's point of view, what's the difference?

At the level of appearances it's simply that the speaker has shifted from presentation to dialogue, from one person speaking to two or more.

Since fear is a psychological affliction, let's ask what change has taken place in the psychology of the speaker to accompany the change in the form of communication. Clearly this is give and take, much closer to pushback than to formal presentation. What happens in the psychology of a speaker who makes that shift?

If we can answer that question, we will learn something about how our enemy operates, in that we'll know what he defines as an opportunity, and we'll know how to render him powerless by denying him his opportunity. And of course we can answer the question.

Every speaker should, though many do not, *sense the audience* as they speak. Study their faces, watch their body language, get inside their heads as Eric Giler tries to do—including learning as much about them as possible before the event. The speaker who fails to do all this, or to do it well enough, places himself at a handicap.

He doesn't know what they need and want, how much they know, what vocabulary they'll respond to—all those elements of audience sensitivity that we covered in Chapter 2. But that's only half of it.

The worst part is that a speaker who is not bonding with his audience is forced back into his own head. This is precisely the place where the vampire takes up his perch. The speaker has in some sense forgotten why he's speaking. He slips into the dead-end concept that his purpose is to give a speech.

So he tries to do just that, and it turns out that he feels a little less than human, a little like a robot who's been wound up in advance, who goes through his paces regardless of what's going on in front of him. No wonder he looks like red meat to the vampire.

Because bugaboo no. 2 for Mr. Fear is *the speaker who's bonding with his audience.* This person is fully aware of both ends of the bond—he is engaged and he cares. The vampire hates him.

If there were only two kinds of speaker in the world, those who care about their audience and those who care about themselves, there's not a shadow of a doubt who the vampire would go for. He'd go after the speaker centered in the foggy dew of his own head.

If I am so centered, I *must* focus on what I've got to lose, what's at stake for *me*, how inexperienced, how fat, how skinny, how dumb, slow, and witless I must seem to *at least one or two* less-than-friendly people in the audience. Or worse, I could be fantasizing about how witty, good-looking, and original I am.

Either way I give myself a dozen things to be frightened about. I am announcing to the vampire, "Look at all I've got to lose!"

Now we can answer the question of what happens to the psychology of the speaker who shifts to dialogue. He gets in touch with his audience in a dozen ways. As he cares more for them, so he cares less for himself. He listens; he feels the blessed relief of human contact.

The speechmaker—a speaker who sees his job as plowing through some predetermined text—stands alone. The man or woman engaging in dialogue makes contact with others and shifts the center outward. To do this you don't have to forget your goals, your identity, your text or argument. All you have to do is remember that you are communicating all that to another person, and the medium of communication is your bond to that other person.

A LITTLE MISTAKE

Let's take a closer look at the poor speechmaker—who is, after all, just like us on a bad day. If we can understand why he's so vulnerable, maybe we can learn from his mistake.

We'll start with that veteran, sixty-year-old speaker who was smitten by fear at a business meeting. He confessed to me later: "I was trying to impress them."

But what's wrong with that? Aren't we all trying to impress the audience one way or another and isn't that what gaining respect and trust are all about?

Yes, but with a difference.

Let's sketch the scene. It was one of those dinner meetings of the MIT Enterprise Forum when entrepreneurs present a business plan and listen to friendly (but real) criticism from an audience of about forty businesspeople. Generally the entrepreneurs are somewhat younger than the audience, somewhat less experienced. Sometimes markedly so. Our sixty-year-old speaker was perhaps thirty years senior to the entrepreneur he was addressing.

His tone was not condescending or patronizing, not in the least, but he raised his hand to speak *for the wrong reason.* In our terms, something was wrong with the psychology of the speaker. Maybe he wasn't being quite honest with himself.

"I had a genuine and, I thought, helpful comment to make," but he wasn't speaking solely to be helpful. "I wanted to show how smart I was." So it wasn't a genuine dialogue and he wasn't bonding with his dialogue partner. He was—this is his word—"strutting."

Some dissonance arose between his proper role of helpful critic and his actual one of performer. In this state of dissonance, he believes, he lost track of his own identity or fell into an identity he couldn't respect. He felt himself veering off into a wrong path. This (in our terms) made him vulnerable to the vampire attack, which duly came, and for the first time in years he had a case of performance anxiety.

The right way to inspire respect and trust, both in the entrepreneur who was supposed to be his dialogue partner and in the audience of spectators to the dialogue, would be to offer truly constructive criticism in a spirit of the search for the best idea. But that wasn't the persuasion goal the confessed strutter had in mind.

The vampire got to him because he opened himself to attack. He opened himself by adopting the wrong goal. (Apparently he is not by nature a strutter.) The goal he adopted was one that shamed him. And guess who saw that his shame made him vulnerable?

Had he chosen to speak for the right reason—to offer real help and useful observations from the perspective of his long experience—he would *automatically* have moved into the dialogue mode, and he would have been immune from fear.

THE FEAR-FIGHTING COMEDIAN

Let's step outside the world of business for a few minutes to get a professional's view on performance anxiety.

Don White is a singer, songwriter and comedian who has conquered his own fear after a years-long struggle. He now gives seminars for singers and other performers, teaching ways to deal with fear. What White teaches is mostly what he's learned by hard experience. You get an idea how seriously he takes the fear thing when you hear him say that he prays before going onstage.

"I ask God to put me in a frame of mind where I'm not thinking about what I have to lose, but what I have to give."

That is his central theme, that there's a wrong way and a right way to define what he's doing when he steps in front of an audience. There is what he calls the selfish way, with the focus on "me" and how he could be "hurt" or diminished. And there's the giving way, with the focus on taking care of the audience.

"The main reason for fear," he said, "is if you wouldn't go out of your way to see your own show." And the way to banish it is to ascend to a level of skill that you can be proud of. Then you don't stand there wondering why all these people have taken it into their heads to come and watch you.

"If you put all your energy into writing a great song, and if you have it and you can say 'I have a great song to give to these people tonight,' then you can say to Mr. Fear, 'Shut up or I'll shoot you.'"

White doesn't go so far as to dress Mr. Fear in a cape and give him brainsucking teeth, but he does personalize him. We've borrowed the name "Mr. Fear" from White.

He says of the old brainsucker, "He has absolutely no redeeming qualities. He's a debilitating and diabolical ass. Declare Mr. Fear an outlaw and greet him whenever possible with gunfire."

Fear destroys what a comedian prizes most: timing, momentum, and delivery. He makes you rush when you should take it easy. He screws you up.

"And there's no way you can trick him away. Gimmicks"—such as imagining the audience undressed—"don't work. The audience is not in their underwear and fear is not stupid." But he's not omnipotent either. What you have to do, White says, is understand your job.

"You cannot be afraid unless you're thinking about yourself—

how can I be hurt, what do I have to lose? It's selfish fear. If you're shaking in your boots, you're thinking about yourself."

And thinking about yourself is not thinking about the job.

"What are people afraid of?" asked White. "Fundamentally the fear means they just don't understand the job. The job is to give to the audience. This is not about what I have to lose, how I can be hurt. It's charity, it's a noble thing.

"It's the kind of thing you look back on at the end of your life and say, 'O.K., there was a moment when I used my assets well.' It's a noble thing to be able to help people along.

"That's why teachers have such a glow about them, the good ones, because it's gift-giving."

He repeated his phrase about taking care of the audience, which he defined as "enriching their lives."

"If you're making the effort to engage the group, you're showing respect. You could just hand out pamphlets but instead you connect personally. When you connect with people, it's the best drug in the world."

THE ENERGY WAVE

There's another view, opposed to White's, on whether Mr. Fear has any redeeming qualities.

Many business speakers, particularly those with several years' experience, feel the fear in their gut and welcome it as a source of energy, a wave they can ride—this is my experience. As long as it's kept at a reasonable amperage, fear or nerves can bring a glow of something very much like joy to a persuader/speaker, especially when the stakes are high.

Many people find that Mr. Fear will never go away altogether. These people tend to depersonalize him. They accept a degree of fear or nervousness about speaking as part of their psychological makeup. They ride the energy wave into and through what is, when all is said and done, a *performance* of a kind.

It is precisely the performance aspect of speaking that scares most people. And it scares them by seeming so far from what they do in everyday life. That's why connecting with the audience takes the speaker out of the fear zone. In a dialogue we not only feel natural, we also set less importance on ourselves.

While Don White's ideas richly deserve the space we have devoted to them, there is another point that calls for comment. It's his use of the word "selfish."

Many speakers are just the opposite of selfish. They are generous and giving by nature, and their fear often arises from this very aspect of their personality. Being generous, being inclined to see what's good and worthy in others, they are all too often inclined to be blind to their own virtues. They underrate themselves.

"These people are sitting there listening to *me*? Why would they waste their time doing that?"

A speaker who has no confidence in himself is not going to be easily persuaded that he has anything to give that the audience wants or needs. Therefore the foundation of a fear-fighting strategy is a justified measure of self-confidence. And this can only be attained by a periodic updating of one's assessment of one's own abilities.

The problem often is that we retain into adulthood attitudes about ourselves that we formed as children. As we grow in knowledge, experience, wisdom, toughness, perseverance, and other virtues, we sometimes fail to notice how much we have changed. Thus a woman of thirty-five may not recognize that she is now the kind of person she admired at twenty.

We all have seen cases like this. We have all experienced those enlightening moments when we realized that we can do today something that was beyond our powers a short time ago. But a self-image is an enduring mindset. And in a business speaker, an undeserved self-image of weakness or incapacity can be an open invitation to Mr. Fear.

A program of periodic self-reassessment is beyond the scope of this book. All we can do here is remark that a great many speakers, perhaps the majority, underrate their performance as speakers, even when they have a strong and justified opinion of their abilities in other areas.

If the vampire flees from the light, it's because he has hardly any power over a mind filled with *the light of knowledge.* A speaker who knows her subject down to the ground may be rattled; she'll never be shut down by fear.

If the vampire flees from a cross, it must be that he can't stand to be near the kind of *solid belief* that lets a person speak to persuade for the best of all reasons, to be useful to others.

And if he casts no image in a mirror, it must be because *he isn't really there.* We make him up. He is *our* bugaboo. He is the creature of our own sense of inadequacy, our misconception of the job, or our isolation from the audience.

To work as speakers and persuaders in the business world, free of interference from this imaginary demon, we need a strategy. Like our basic persuasion strategy it must be simple, clear, and bold. Since fear is a highly personal problem, each speaker must evolve his or her own strategy; but here's a suggestion:

Work to achieve. Take confidence from your achievements. When you persuade, connect with your audience as one human being offering a benefit to another.

If you live this strategy you'll make a very unappealing target for the brainsucker.

7

The Good Persuader
and the Good Life

Business is more than making a living. Like medicine, law, and the ministry; like military service; like charities and other nonprofits; and like professional sports, *business is an arena of personal endeavor.*

Men and women go into it to make widgets and money, to make an impact, to avoid loneliness and stimulate their brain, to give refreshing exercise to their social instincts. This multitude of incentives, and many others, including sometimes a lack of anything else to do, drive people into business.

Many arrived puzzled. What's this all about and what am I doing here? They are soon required to learn the first two tangible measures of success in the business life—production and profit. How many widgets did we make? Were they any good? Did we make them efficiently? And, was the enterprise profitable?

They learn the third measure perhaps more gradually. This one is less tangible but equally significant. There are those who claim it's the only one that matters. This third measure of success is called "human flourishing." It is the full development and deployment of the energies and talents of the person, working with and against others in the social setting we call competition.

Taken together, *production, profit,* and *flourishing* form a pretty good answer to the question, What am I doing here? Anybody who devotes himself to producing useful goods or services, who plays his part in making the profits that draw investment and sustain the enterprise, and who feels himself extending his abilities has good reason to be satisfied.

Perfect satisfaction undoubtedly eludes us all, but these three measures help us to assess our progress toward that level of satisfaction that's open to us this side of Paradise.

This book has been about one of the three measures—human flourishing. And so we conclude by examining briefly how persuasive speech aids flourishing.

A young man called Dan went into the creative side of advertising straight out of college. Six months into his first job he put together a direct-mail project that won him a prestigious award and an offer from a big league agency. He took the offer.

The company was growing almost exponentially, adding dream clients and staff weekly, providing Dan with as many opportunities as he could seize. He did seize them. He had a tremendous flow of ideas and a gift for their practical application.

The beginning of the application phase is to sell the idea in-house, and he proved adept at that too. Steadily, deservedly, he got better accounts and more responsibility. He was promoted to vice president and creative director of an affiliated company by the age of thirty.

If "flourishing" applies to anybody, it applied to him. He was exercising his creative talents to their full range and constantly meeting new opportunities to expand and renew them. He was getting what we all—or nearly all—desire, due recognition of his achievements. He was making good money and adding responsibilities, moving into administrative and leadership roles while still keeping his creative talents active.

He was, and still is, a living definition of the flourishing professional:

- Vigorously active in his chosen field;
- Facing new challenges and problems every day;
- Exercising his own talents to the fullest and helping his colleagues to do the same;
- Winning the appreciation of his superiors for his role in building the company and adding and retaining clients.

■ ■ ■

This is still a happy story. We are not building up to some calamity, but to a new challenge, perhaps the hardest yet.

He found that at the level of V.P./creative director the client audiences he faced were tougher, more skeptical, more acutely conscious of how much money was on the table. They were also, usually, much older than he, and inclined to wonder if anybody so young could possibly know anything they didn't. There was an attitude of, We're the big guys. Who the hell are you?

This kind of pressure can be crippling. It didn't cripple Dan but he admits to moments when he wondered—maybe they're right. What *do* I know anyway? But his confidence was sufficient to the task. He kept going. He saw the new kind of audience, with its new kind of resistance, as simply the latest of the challenges he had faced in a steady series since the beginning of his career.

But this kind of pressure has two sources, from two kinds of audience—external and internal, the audience drawn from client companies and the one drawn from one's own company. The speaker knows he represents more than himself alone. He represents his team's idea. He represents all their arduous, accumulated effort and all they have invested in their work product. He carries their hopes in his hands.

And when the conferees have gathered and the door closes, when the players sit down and begin the round of introductions, the speaker—Dan—must not only convince the skeptical Mr. Big from a Fortune 100 company. He must convince his own boss, sitting beside him, that it was no mistake to put him there.

As you have already guessed, this is a true story and it isn't over yet. "Dan" is turning his extraordinarily able mind to the job of winning from a client audience the respect and trust his superiors have placed in him—and proving them right.

What hangs in the balance?

Well—plenty. There are a dozen ways to say it—money, position, vindication, pride—but all can be summed up in a word: *flourishing.*

It is more than success. One can succeed in an effort so thick with compromise and betrayal that a good clean failure would look like pure happiness. And one can fail in a magnificent effort that somehow brings its own redemption.

If Dan should fail at this new level, he won't be ruined. He'll still be the richly talented man who got so far so fast. But imagine if he should succeed . . .

Cicero, the Roman advocate we mentioned a while back, said that learning the arts of persuasive speech was not a matter of collecting a bag of tricks. Rather it was a task of developing the whole person.

This is a fully convincing idea. Tricks do not persuade us, certainly not in the long run. Men and women do. And the best persuaders, the ones we not only agree with but admire, are the ones, like Susan Angelastro, like Harry, who somehow convey the feeling that they're *all there*—whole, developed, well-integrated personalities.

Now let's try something original. Let's take Cicero's proposition and turn it around. Could it be that a person who consciously develops her or his ability to persuade moves, by that very effort, toward a better integrated and more complete self?

A daring, maybe a crazy idea. Certainly some businesspeople manage to persuade others by stealth and falsehood. But suppose a man or woman—suppose Dan, for example—were to take seriously such concepts as Subject Mastery and Empathy, were to respect his audience enough to devote real study to it, were to search for the goals that confer the greatest benefit.

Suppose he were to frame his arguments with due respect for the soundness of the evidence and reasoning.

And suppose he "pushed back" where he felt a real and honest doubt about an opposing thesis.

Supposing all this, it doesn't seem quite so crazy that somebody like Dan would develop to a higher degree both his intellectual and human qualities to the point where those around him, and he himself, would notice a difference—a new luster to an already appealing and impressive persona.

If Dan succeeds at his new level—if any of us succeeds in meeting a comparable challenge—

Let's leave that sentence right where it is. It's as good a way as any to bring the book to a close, and to wish the reader a flourishing life of professional and personal fulfillment.

Acknowledgments

I am deeply indebted to two people and one institution.

To Robert W. Kent, former head of management communication at the Harvard Business School, for hiring me to teach oral presentation and sharing his knowledge of the art.

To Phyllis Strimling, head of the management program at Radcliffe Seminars, for giving me any number of chances to teach and learn from a fully engaged and dynamic group of students.

And to the MIT Enterprise Forum of Cambridge, Inc., for providing scores of learning opportunities, always keyed to the business experience of the participants.

Among the many men and women whose knowledge enlivens the Forum's programs, I would like to mention two. Jim Geisman and Bob Anderson, it seems to me, exemplify all that's best about the Forum—a keen empathy for the entrepreneurs who present their business plans and problems to it, deep knowledge of the intricacies as well as the broad concepts of business operations, and tough but fair criticism of the kind we all need but seldom get from our friends.

Many of the businesspeople whose ideas and experience enrich this book have served on the Forum's boards and led its seminars. Their work brought a variety of business examples and viewpoints to my attention.

And my clients, whether I work with them in seminars or individually, have also sharpened my thinking and opened new perspectives for me on the art of persuasion.

My friends Leigh Hafrey and Eugene Mihaly read and criticized parts of the manuscript in its earliest stages of development. I am happy to take this opportunity both to thank them and to clear them of any responsibility for such errors and omissions as may persist in the completed book.

At Houghton Mifflin, the team of Alan Andres, Marnie Cochran, and Lisa Sacks performed up to the highest professional standard. I am grateful to them and deeply respectful.

My daughters, Liza and Zoe, and their husbands, Bryan Loofbourrow and Matt Groom, have helped in a variety of ways. I thank them sincerely. I wish also to thank my sister-in-law, Sharon Pfarrer, entrepreneur, for offering an instructive description of her business.

While hundreds of men and women have given freely of their time and observations, I am especially grateful to Susan Angelastro, Scott Barnum, Corey Darling, Eric Giler, Shannon Gilligan, James Groom, Susan Hammond, Ian Just, Barbara A. Piette, John A. Pope Jr., Stephen Ricci, Dave Rothfeld, Diane Rochat, Sheila Sinclair, Joseph W. Shoquist, Christopher L. Stevens, Don White, Sarah Woolverton, and Mitko Zagoroff.

Finally I wish to acknowledge my debt to my partner, Anne Just, for her acute criticism, her optimism, and her dear companionship.

Jay Conrad Levinson's
Guerrilla Marketing International

From the success of the Guerrilla Marketing books sprang Jay Conrad Levinson's Guerrilla Marketing International (1986), a company founded on the understanding that most businesses are not IBM or AT&T and don't have huge marketing budgets to work with, a company organized with the purpose of helping businesses learn to use the power of guerrilla marketing instead of the brute force of enormous budgets.

To learn more about Guerrilla Marketing services and products, write, call, or e-mail Guerrilla Marketing International, P.O. Box 1336, Mill Valley, CA 94942. 415-381-8361.

Now You Can Continue to Be a Guerrilla Marketer with The Guerrilla Marketing Newsletter!

Now you can continue being an informed Guerrilla Marketer with *The Guerrilla Marketing Newsletter*. It provides you with state-of-the-moment marketing tips and insights to maximize your business profits.

To subscribe to *The Guerrilla Marketing Newsletter*, call 800-748-6444. The subscription rate is $59 a year for 6 issues.

Get the Complete Guerrilla Arsenal!

Guerrilla Marketing: Secrets for Making Big Profits from Your Small Business   ISBN 0-395-64496-8

The book that started the Guerrilla Marketing revolution, now completely revised and updated for the nineties. Full of the latest strategies, information on the latest technologies, new programs for targeted prospects, and management lessons for the twenty-first century.

Guerrilla Financing: Alternative Techniques to Finance Any Small Business   ISBN 0-395-52264-1

The ultimate sourcebook for finance in the 1990s, and the first book to describe in detail all the traditional and alternative sources of funding for small and medium-size businesses.

***Guerrilla Marketing Attack: New Strategies, Tactics, and Weapons
for Winning Big Profits***   ISBN 0-395-50220-9

A companion to *Guerrilla Marketing,* this book arms small and medium-size businesses with vital information about direct marketing, customer relations, cable TV, desktop publishing, ZIP code inserts, TV shopping networks, and much more.

***Guerrilla Marketing Excellence: The Fifty Golden Rules for
Small-Business Success***   ISBN 0-395-60844-9

Jay Levinson delivers the 50 basic truths of guerrilla marketing which can make or break your company, including the crucial difference between profits and sales, marketing in a recession, and the latest uses of video and television to assure distribution.

***Guerrilla Selling: Unconventional Weapons and Tactics for
Increasing Your Sales***   ISBN 0-395-57820-5

Today's increasingly competitive business environment requires new skills and commitment from salespeople. *Guerrilla Selling* presents unconventional selling tactics that are essential for success.

The Guerrilla Marketing Handbook   ISBN 0-395-70013-2

The Guerrilla Marketing Handbook presents Jay Levinson's entire arsenal of marketing weaponry, including a step-by-step guide to developing a marketing campaign and detailed descriptions of more than 100 marketing tools.

***Guerrilla Advertising: Cost-Effective Tactics for Small-Business
Success***   ISBN 0-395-68718-9

Jay Levinson applies his proven guerrilla philosophy to advertising. Teeming with anecdotes about past and current advertising successes and failures, the book entertains as it teaches the nuts and bolts of advertising for small businesses.

Guerrilla Marketing for the Home-Based Business
ISBN 0-395-74283-8

Usually undercapitalized and short on relevant marketing know-how, home-based businesses have specific marketing needs. Using case studies, anecdotes, illustrations, and examples, guerrilla marketing gurus Jay Levinson and Seth Godin present practical, accessible, and inspirational marketing advice and the most effective arsenal of marketing tools for America's fastest-growing business segment.

Guerrilla Marketing Online Weapons (second edition)
ISBN 0-395-86061-X

Here are 100 online marketing strategies to help businesses take advantage of the Internet's great marketing potential. From e-mail addresses and signatures to storefronts, feedback mechanisms, electronic catalogs, and press kits, *Guerrilla Marketing Online Weapons* will help any business, small or large, define, refine, and put its message on the Net with ease.

The Way of the Guerrilla   ISBN 0-395-77018-1

An invaluable blueprint for future business success, including advice for both new and seasoned entrepreneurs on everything from preparing a focused mission statement and hiring responsible employees to delegating, finding more time for family and the community, and sustaining one's passion for work. By following *The Way of the Guerrilla*, enlightened and successful entrepreneurs will discover that a balanced life is the means to achieving emotional and financial success, now and in the century to come.

Guerrilla Marketing Online (second edition)   ISBN 0-395-86061-X

From getting acquainted to Internet culture to creating a complete online marketing plan, *Guerrilla Marketing Online* offers the basic training entrepreneurs need to take Jay Levinson's proven marketing tactics to the new and important marketplace of the Internet.

These titles are available through bookstores, or you can order directly from Houghton Mifflin at 1-800-225-3362.